10th November 1999

Animal Tales

ANIMAL TALES

**The Adventures of
Wildlife Photographer
Andy Rouse**

**Designed & Edited by
Grant Bradford**

GREEN MAN
BOOKS

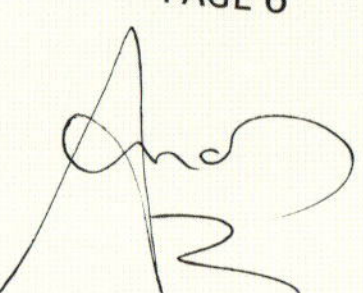

An Expedition to Japan

The Red Fox

The Water Giants

The Grizzly Bear

Photographic Details

the Orang Utan

Welcome to Animal Tales, a unique collection of the trials and tribulations of being a wildlife photographer. Don't worry though, this isn't a standard photography book, it's for animal lovers of all ages. My philosophy regarding wildlife is simple, I don't want to stand miles away staring at some hairy beast through some paparazzi style monster lens; I want to be up close and personal, staring it straight in the eye and feeling that adrenalin rush of uncertainty.

I've always managed to get myself into dodgy situations with animals, possibly the worst incidents have been nearly being trodden on by a short sighted geriatric elephant, a polar bear that ran straight at my snowmobile or when a crocodile snapped its jaws so close to my face I could smell its breath. The worst injuries I have suffered however are when a particularly playful badger sank its teeth firmly into my backside and a spider bit me malevolently where I'd rather not be bitten!

In the first chapter of this book you will see how my fascination with pushing myself to the limits really started; a daytime madness, induced by either the sun or too much of the falling down juice, convinced me that laying down under an advancing elephant was a great idea. This is followed by the ultimate thrill, enticing a South American crocodile called a Caiman to snap its jaws next to my face using a piranha as bait.

The next two sections show some really extreme photography; stalking a lioness in the grass with a blanket on my head (before you ask, I still don't know why I did this) and snowmobiling after polar bears in the frozen Arctic. This is perhaps the section I like best, as not only does it show my favourite animal, but gives you an insight into what life is like dealing with extreme elements in the wild.
After that its a small section on the delights of Japan other than Sushi and comfortable shoes, and then back home to the story of how I raised four orphan fox cubs and released them back into the wild.

Finally the book rounds off with three small but action packed sections.
You will see how getting too close to a hippo can be a life threatening experience, how some bears just can't get the hang of fishing, and how an Orang-utan called Christine took such a shine to me that she washed my hair! So come with me and experience nature though my eyes.

ENCOUNTERS with ELEPHANTS

The elephant's tusk is really an overgrown incisor. They grow continuously to a length of 2.5-3 metres and can weigh in excess of 60 kg a piece. The tusks have many uses; digging food from the ground, to show aggression and in serious fights between competing Bulls. Fortunately I used a long lens to get this close-up of an old tusker, his malevolent look convinced me that I made the right choice.

Elephants have beautiful toenails. Not exactly an earth-shattering revelation but one which I can vouch for from personal experience. I don't really know what possessed me to lay down in the grass underneath a 10 ton 75 year old bull elephant, but I did. Perhaps it was the lure of hard cash, the accolades from my peers or a career on television gameshows. More likely it's because I'm a complete nutter.

Half an hour earlier it had seemed like a cool thing to do. I've always loved to get in close to animals rather than watching them from a distance quietly sipping a G&T; when my guide Gavin Blair gave me a challenge I had no choice but to accept. I relish challenges *(such as assembling flat packed furniture)* and lying down getting an eye-level view of an elephants toenails was one that I just couldn't resist. "Don't worry" Gavin said "they're old guys and have seen it all before". Quite whether they'd seen a skinny wildlife photographer lying down beneath them was questionable but I trusted Gavin with my life. So, pockets loaded with film and my quietest camera in hand, I jumped down from the safety of the jeep and made my way across the grass...

The Elephant is the largest and heaviest animal on land and it is spread across Africa south of the Sahara.

Elephants come down to drink in the middle of the day, using well defined paths to get from their jungle feeding areas. These paths are usually very straight, and when viewed from the air you can see that they are the quickest way of getting from A to B. Perhaps the Romans learnt a thing or two about road building from elephants.

The waterhole we had chosen, already had several elephants drinking happily around it, and more were on their way from the forest. They all seemed to use the same path and so it was the natural place for me to lurk.

The Bull Elephant strode closer, tusks in the air to show he was annoyed, and I wondered if my decision to leave the computer industry had been a wise one.

ONE MORE STEP...

I chose a nice spot about two metres from the path and laid down to wait. I spied my first victims in the distance heading in my general direction but I knew from experience that they'd take an awfully long time to get to me. Elephants move at a very very stately pace, and don't rush for anyone. So I had plenty of time to consider the rashness of what I was doing.

The first elephant got to within 30 feet and suddenly became aware that he was not alone in the grass. They don't have great eyesight *(because they are hopeless at keeping appointments with Opticians and the glasses fall off their trunks)* but he knew something strange was there. For all he knew I could have been a predator and he reacted accordingly. His trunk went up in the air,

raising his tusks in an aggressive posture and he let out an ear-splitting bellow. His ears flapped around throwing dust into the air and generally adding to the feeling that I'd made a grave error of judgement.

He stepped closer and closer, by now the sky was full of elephant. The trumpeting continued but by now I'd had a major sense of humour failure and so failed to appreciate its musical qualities. It's one thing hearing that sound from a distance, but quite another when its a deafening 20 feet away and directed straight at me. There was no way I could outrun him so I just lay there, trying to calmly remind myself that he was a Bull Elephant, and not a dangerous female with young. He crossed his legs, relaxed a little and began to sniff me with his trunk, which was almost touching me as by now he was ridiculously close.

I remember laying there and looking straight at his toe nails, as they were at my eye level. They were polished and whilst looking at them I noticed for the first time how the bottom of his feet spread out like cushions every time he took a step. He had built in shock-absorbers and I realised the more I looked him up and down what a wonderful creation he was. He was so close I had to crane my neck to look up at him but by now he had become very inquisitive and tolerated my little movements.

Just as we were getting totally relaxed, his friends turned up. Its always the same when you have a party, someone brings uninvited guests who usually have tattoos and drink all your beer. Clearly his friends wanted to join in and five minutes later I had three elephants towering over me. I was the centre of attention, being watched by three huge old guys for whom the encounter with Andy Rouse must have been the highlight *(don' t you mean lowlight – ed.)* of their week. But at this point I did get very nervous. If a single elephant had got nasty then I convinced myself that I could dodge it and do my best to get out of its way. With three I didn't have a chance and decided I was skinny enough without being trod on by an elephant. So I stopped taking pictures, lay flat, and pretended to be as uninteresting as possible. After five tense minutes the lead elephant, obviously bored with the sideshow and getting thirstier by the minute, huffed and sauntered off. I actually felt the ground move underneath me as his two friends followed him, leaving a very relieved and sweaty wildlife photographer in the grass.

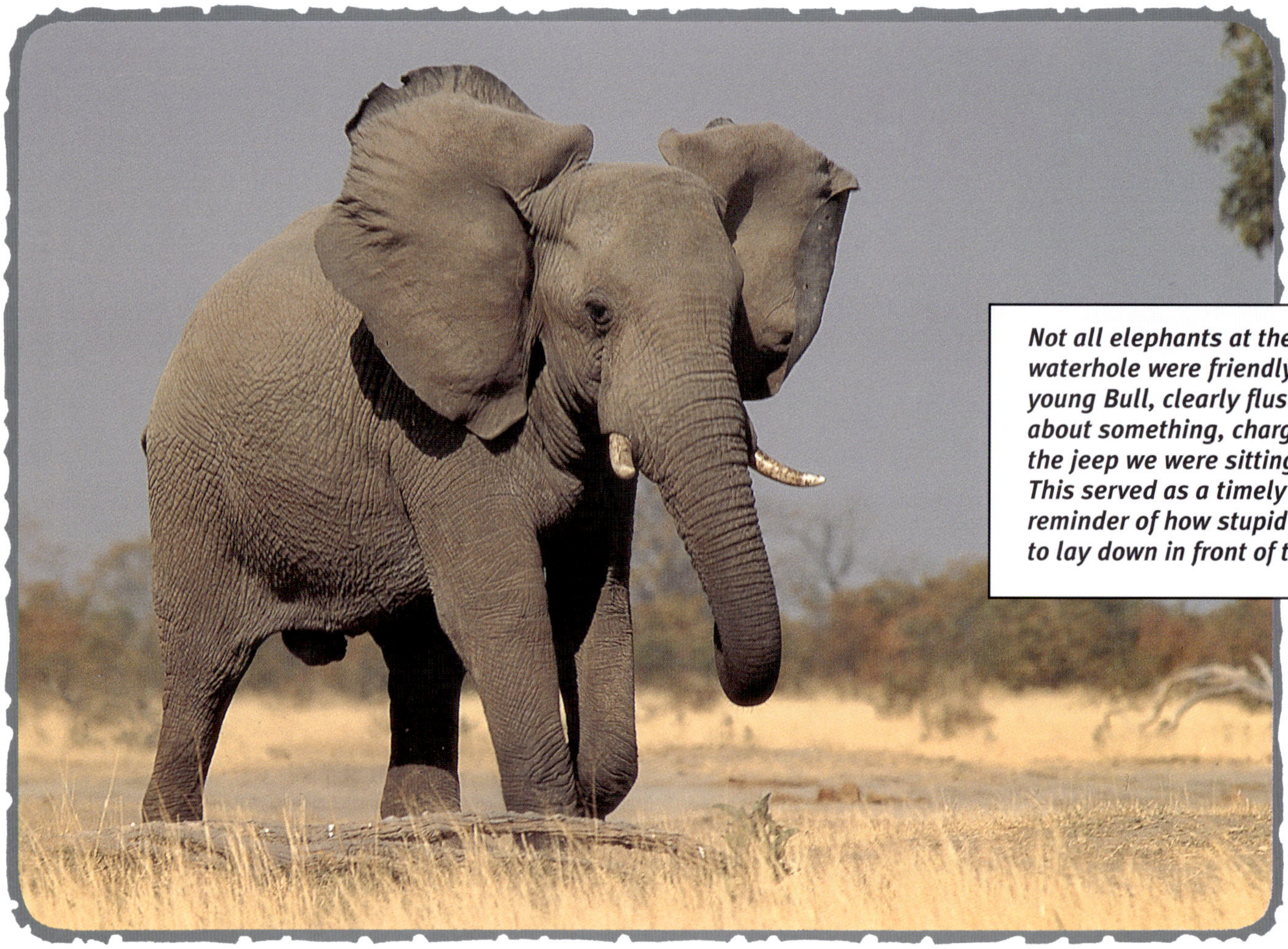

Not all elephants at the waterhole were friendly. This young Bull, clearly flustered about something, charged the jeep we were sitting in. This served as a timely reminder of how stupid it was to lay down in front of them.

The Elephant is the largest land animal and big bulls can weigh in excess of 5000 kg. To maintain this size they must eat 150-175 kg of grass and foliage per day. They are superbly adapted for getting a wide variety of food, as they have the most versatile feeding utensil in the animal kingdom – their trunk. This is a muscular tube, with two small "fingers" at the end which are used to grab small objects like photographers. The flexibility of the trunk allows them to grasp huge amounts of grass in one go, or reach higher into the trees for prime fruit and leaves than any other herbivore. I once saw an elephant use its trunk against a tree to shake the fruit from it. As you'll see later, the trunk is a complex piece of machinery to work and young elephants don't master it for quite some time.

Believe me when I tell you that elephants can run. Their normal "I'll get there eventually" walking speed is about 4mph, which even I could match. This can quickly turn into a 20 mph sprint when annoyed, something which the fastest athlete in the world would fail to match. Perhaps there should be a new Olympic event – Elephant racing. Just like greyhound racing when the greyhounds chase the hare, in this new Olympic sport, the elephants would chase the athletes. I think that we'd have lots more world records broken, although catching the elephants at the end might prove a little difficult.

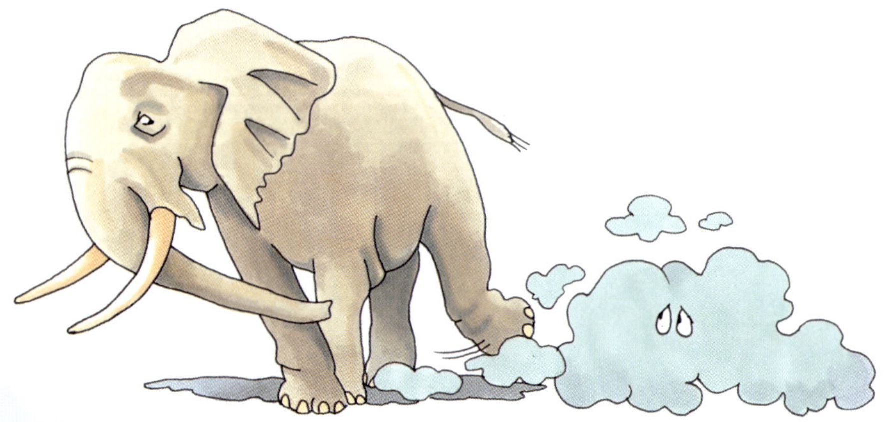

Elephants have a remarkable knack of doing the unexpected. After my experiences at the waterhole the previous day, I tried the whole thing again at another waterhole. This time the elephant became very aggressive as it got closer and trumpeted like I'd never heard before. Still not sure if I was lion or quivering human wreck he drew up his chest (quite a feat for an elephant) and kicked dirt in my face. Now, I've had dirt kicked in my face on beaches the world over, so all this succeeded in doing was making me burst out laughing. I think it broke the ice between us, or more likely it allowed him to see I was human, and he noticeably relaxed. Trust me to pick an elephant with bad eyesight!

AT THE WATERHOLE

I'd been sitting down quite happily next to a waterhole snapping away when a very inquisitive old guy came over and started checking me out. Most of the regulars there were used to me by now and didn't pay me a second glance, but he was obviously a new elephant on the scene and considered me a novelty. Thinking that there was every chance of becoming a pancake, I crawled backwards so that my legs were under the jeep; in reality the elephant could quite easily lift the jeep to get to me but I figured he didn't fancy me that much. My movement clearly re-kindled his interest as he came and stood right in front of me, blocking out all sight of the other elephants.

Elephants need to drink huge amounts of water to survive; typically they will drink about 100 litres at one go. This particular part of Africa is very dry and because of this, the distances between waterholes are vast. This means that only the bulls can survive here, the breeding herds which contain the youngsters prefer to stay near to permanent water to make it possible for the calves to drink.

I was just about to use some choice phrases that you shouldn't use in front of elephants, when I saw that he'd perfectly framed the others through his legs. Most people when they hang a picture on the wall use a frame to surround the picture, me no I have to be different, I use an elephant!

One of the joys of working with elephants is that they are so unpredictable. One evening we saw a particularly large bull strolling across the plains at dusk towards a waterhole. I tried the "lay down and hope technique" but soon realised with horror that he had no intention of stopping. I didn't want to be flattened and decided to get the hell out of there – believe me I broke the Olympic sprint record running away! I'd made two bad assumptions – that elephants can see in the dark and that all elephants find Andy Rouse interesting! Still, it was a nice picture and I particularly love the raggedy ears which are a sign of his great age.

Baby Elephants have no control over their trunks as it takes a couple of years to be able to master the 200 muscles needed to move them. I watched, ashamedly I have to admit in fits of laughter, as this little chap got completely stuck in a mud wallow. Each time he tried to get out he'd invariably stand on his trunk, lose his balance and slide all the way back down into the wallow. After a while a female elephant, probably his mother, took pity on the rapidly tiring little guy and helped him out with a shove from her trunk. Everyone needs a little helping hand sometimes!

You might be wondering why elephants go to all this bother to cover themselves in mud. There are two reasons. The first is to protect their skin from overheating in the harsh sun. The second is to stop being bitten by the legions of insects that follow them everywhere, it seems amazing to me that such a large animal would actually feel it!

SPLATTER

Elephants are shy bathers, especially when they are using a mud wallow. I'd tried lying down next to the wallow to get a shot, but each time the elephant would steadfastly refuse to perform whilst I was anywhere near it. I guess you can hardly blame them as you'd be a little perturbed if you emerged from your bathroom and found me with a camera outside. Clearly I'd have to be a little sneaky to get the shot, but that's my middle name (actually it's Stephen but that's not my fault).

I'm a great believer in modern technology and I use all kinds of gizmos to get unusual pictures. This time I decided to use an infra-red trigger to fire the camera remotely, which I hoped the elephant would be more willing to accept. So I buried my camera in the mud surrounding the wallow, attached the trigger and checked the view through the camera, as I wouldn't be able to change my mind once the elephant was happily chucking mud over itself.

A second elephant appeared and boldly walked straight into the centre of the wallow. It scooped up a large trunkful of mud and in a deft movement, sprayed it all over its back and side. I let him do this a few times before taking any pictures; all was going to plan until he heard the sound of the camera winding on the next shot. He immediately stopped his wallowing, stared at the offending object and stretched his trunk out to sense any tell-tale smell. I'm sure that I saw a mischievous look in his eye, and as he scooped up another trunkful of mud I somehow knew that everything was about to go pear shaped.

As he raised his trunk I pressed my trigger and the camera started taking pictures, just at the moment when the elephant let fly with the mud. It hit the camera with a resounding splat, sending the whole lot rocking backwards. Obviously satisfied and now assured of complete privacy, the elephant carried on with his mudbath, leaving me speechless *(for once!)*.

I knew that film would be special and for the rest of the trip kept it in a separate pocket – I even slept with it under my pillow.
When I got back to England I drove straight to my friend Andrew's lab in Wales to get it developed. For the next two hours I was like a cat on a hot tin roof, pacing up and down and generally getting in everyone's way. Just as I was in danger of being seriously injured by the staff, the processor beeped at me and started spewing out my developed film. I virtually ripped it out of the machine (in hindsight hardly the best thing to do with a valuable film), scanned each image carefully and let out a shriek when I saw the image that you see here. Andrew, fearing that I would damage it in my excitement, sensibly took it away from me and made a copy for me to drool over.

Somehow I'd managed to capture the mud as it was inches from hitting the lens. The real bonus in the picture was the sleeping elephant by the tree who was waiting patiently in line for the wallow. It was the shot that I'd dreamt of getting, possibly the most original and unusual shot of an elephant ever taken. It went on to win the prestigious Animal Behaviour category in the 1998 BBC / BG Wildlife Photographer of the Year Competition. My proudest moment was standing on stage at the Natural History Museum in London receiving my award from Sir David Attenborough. As I walked onto the stage he told me that it was the most amazing shot he had ever seen of an elephant; there's no better praise than that. Proof that trying something unusual can sometimes be rewarding, even if my camera was ruined in the process.

As the elephants got closer I could see several babies in between their mothers' legs; it was a breeding herd and that meant trouble for the Hippos.

The lead elephant, not wanting to take any risks with the youngsters in the herd, charged the group of hippos.

The river boiled as 20 hippos leapt into it. They congregated in the centre, grunting defiance but knowing they had lost the battle.

DOWN BY THE RIVER

One of the things that I love about this job, apart from wearing all the kinky camouflage clothing, is that I get to see things in the natural world that are unique. One of my strongest memories came with elephants in Africa, late one June afternoon. I'd spent the afternoon sitting across the river from a group of Hippos; it was hot and they were merrily snoring away. Then, in the distance, I saw some elephants approaching; nothing surprising about that as it was hot and they were coming down to drink. Unfortunately for the hippos, they were heading in their direction, although of course the hippos were blissfully unaware of anything. The lead female elephant, probably the matriarch, trumpeted a warning, the sound breaking the fragile silence of the river. It had a remarkable effect on the hippos. Woken from their sleep, they turned and challenged the elephants. Big mistake.

With the hippos taken care of, the elephants started the serious business of drinking. The babies, as always, didn't quite get the idea and used the time to spray water over any unsuspecting adult. For a few moments all was peace and calm, then I heard another trumpet in the distance. Through the trees another breeding herd was approaching – this was going to be worse than a local soccer match. The herd already at the river all raised their trunks to smell the newcomers, and I could see through the dust that the new arrivals had done the same. They came together in an uneasy silence, the lead elephant of the new herd taking a slightly wider path to bring her herd slightly further up river.

Through the clouds of golden dust I could see another herd approaching.

The newcomers raised their trunks in the air to help catch any scent that might identify the herd already at the river.

Elephants are very social animals and have a ranking system with the matriarch at the top, followed by the older females, then all the way down to the youngsters. I watched as one bold youngster came right up to the new herd, trunk raised, and sniffed one of the larger females. As the lower ranked elephant it put its trunk up towards the females mouth, but it was so short that it couldn't reach. It was a beautiful moment, both of them silhouetted by the dust and the setting sun.

Steam was now pouring from my camera as I tried to record the scene as best I could. Failure would mean I should be locked up for the rest of my natural life, with nothing but my awful singing for company. So I used about 60 rolls of film *(half of my allowance for the 3 week trip)* in less than an hour, trying to do the scene justice.

Water cascaded from the elephant's mouth, the setting sun highlighting it like crystal.

The river-bank was now packed with elephants as far as the eye could see.

It was becoming the social place to be, and two more breeding herds had turned up to drink. I know that women find me irresistible (oh yeah, I wish) but this was getting silly. The air was now thick with orange dust and the elephants were silhouettes against the setting sun. At that moment I decided that photography was not the most important thing in my life and put my camera down. When you're taking pictures so intently it's hard to watch and enjoy what you are seeing, this was now my time to just enjoy the spectacle.

At the peak time the river was lined with drinking elephants as far as I could see in both directions.

The only sounds that I could hear were elephants drinking; they seemed to suck up the whole river before noisily squirting it into their mouths. Then, as if by command, the elephants started melting back into the forest. After a few minutes, apart from a few shapes moving through the dust, the river was silent again. The hippos, clearly still a little angry at having their afternoon siesta so violently disturbed, snorted loudly at the retreating elephants.
I decided it was time to leave before they took it out on me.

And so all the herds left and the river became quiet again, that is, apart from the hippos grunting away.

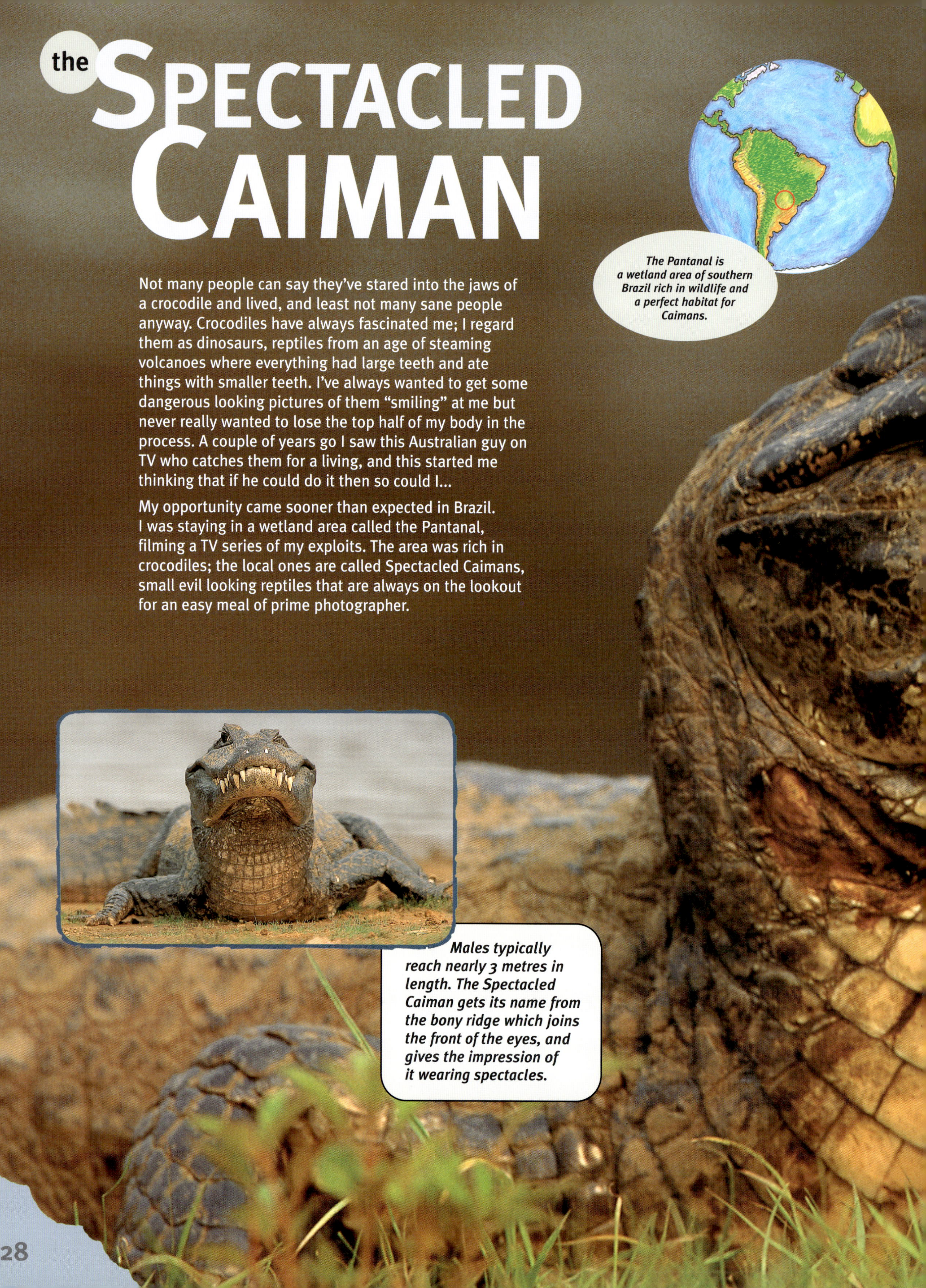

the SPECTACLED CAIMAN

Not many people can say they've stared into the jaws of a crocodile and lived, and least not many sane people anyway. Crocodiles have always fascinated me; I regard them as dinosaurs, reptiles from an age of steaming volcanoes where everything had large teeth and ate things with smaller teeth. I've always wanted to get some dangerous looking pictures of them "smiling" at me but never really wanted to lose the top half of my body in the process. A couple of years go I saw this Australian guy on TV who catches them for a living, and this started me thinking that if he could do it then so could I...

My opportunity came sooner than expected in Brazil. I was staying in a wetland area called the Pantanal, filming a TV series of my exploits. The area was rich in crocodiles; the local ones are called Spectacled Caimans, small evil looking reptiles that are always on the lookout for an easy meal of prime photographer.

Caimans hang around our ranch in the Pantanal all the time, you only have to step into a boat when a pair of eyes breaks the surface to check you out. Caimans float like this so that they can see and smell what is around them, whilst still allowing them to make a quick getaway by diving.

The ranch where I stay is a beautiful place, on the bend of a river with jungle on all sides. Several Caiman hang out in the bay waiting for unsuspecting animals to walk by and I've spent quite a few evenings talking away to them about anything that enters my head whilst sipping a local beer. They all raise their heads and listen when I talk, which makes a nice change, although they do always want to talk politics.

I hatched a cunning plan to photograph Caimans which would also look good on TV; I was going to lay on the edge of the water and use fish bait to get them to come right up to me with their jaws open. Sitting in the comfort of my office now it sounds like I'd drunk too much of the falling down juice, but at the time it seemed perfectly sensible (next time I'll wear a sun hat more of the time).

I chose a bayou off the main river that had more Caimans in it than a James Bond movie. Caimans are always hungry and can't resist an easy meal such as fish, or Andy's arm. The first step was to get some fish to use as bait. Fishing Brazilian style is to put a little bit of meat on a line and hang it over the edge of the boat. Do we catch carp or trout? No, we get piranha. Yep, those little nightmares with snapping teeth that would happily account for your toes and fingers, are prime and much favoured Caiman food.

The piranha bait soon attracted Caimans from everywhere and before I knew it there were several within striking distance of my face. During one attempt to snatch the bait, a Caiman managed to bite the one next to it. The smaller guy took it well, which is a good job as Caiman have been known to be cannibalistic in times of hardship. Oh great, I didn't think it could get any worse, of course it did...

TOOTHY AND FRIENDS

Xavier, my guide, returned triumphantly with a handful of snapping piranhas and I took up my position, prone at the waters edge. It was a strange feeling being at the Caimans' eye level, they didn't share my misgivings and simply stared back at me from the centre of the lagoon. To get their attention *(ermm, did we really want to do this)* Xavier cast the piranha out beyond them and quickly reeled the line back like a champion fisherman. The piranha sped between the caiman and suddenly the bayou was all tails and teeth. Caimans started coming down every bank and the ones in the water started making rapid progress in my direction. Xavier smiled with success, then dangled the piranha about two feet in front of me.

The first caiman steamed in, its' mouth opening to reveal two sets of razor sharp teeth that were used entirely too regularly for my liking. Through my camera it looked awesome, it was only when I looked directly with my eyes that I realised that toothy was two feet from my face. It snapped at the piranha a few times, Xavier pulling it away just in time, but I'm sure one reptilian eye was kept firmly on me.

It surprised me how quickly the Caiman could strike, one second they were staring longingly at the bait, the next they were carrying it off in their mouths. Hopefully my leg would be a bit more than they could manage.

It was all going well when suddenly disaster struck. The piranha, which had been in Toothy's jaws, sprang loose and landed on the ground next to my face. Toothy and I stared at each other for a few seconds, sizing up each others intentions; his were simple – food, mine were to find the ejector seat button or the trap door lever that would remove me from this nightmare. Our growing friendship was interrupted by a larger caiman who, watching from the sidelines, had decided it wanted the piranha badly. It came steaming out of the water at me, mouth wide open and I threw myself backwards, landing with a crash on my rucksack.

The caiman grabbed the fish in its jaws, and for good measure made a snap at my trailing foot. My football career was saved by the fact that it not only had a jawful of piranha, but that caiman cannot bite straight on and have to turn sideways to do it. Satisfied, the caiman retreated with the fish, a disconcerting crunching sound coming from its mouth as it crushed the piranha in its jaws. I felt exhilarated, and for several hours was on a real high. I'd seen the Caiman at both extremes of its life, silent hunter and merciless killer, looked deep into the jaws of a dinosaur and still kept all my limbs. Tyrannosaurus Rex here I come.

Although I knew Toothy was just after the fish, there was something evil about the way it looked at me down the side of its open jaws. Adult Caiman are able to drag adult pigs into the water, so my humble physique would present few problems to it.

This picture of a magnificent male lion standing over its kill tells a big lie – the male lion didn't actually make the kill. He was probably dozing under some shady tree somewhere whilst the pride females did all the hard work. As soon as he knows a kill has been made, and the bush telegraph of vultures and hyenas will tell him that, he'll amble along and try to get a free meal. The King of the Beasts is really nature's greatest scrounger!

The KING of BEASTS

I'm a very commercial wildlife photographer and have to take pictures that sell. I'd love to take arty pictures, you know the ones where the photographer says that they come from their innermost self, expressing a post nationalistic feeling of inner city life of... Anyway you get the idea. Take the picture opposite and the one below as examples. One is very popular with clients and one most certainly isn't.

My personal favourite is the male lion standing dominant over the Buffalo, a real king of the beasts picture. It won't sell in most countries because it has blood round its mouth and shows death, despite the fact that this is reality and lions don't eat broccoli. The other picture is altogether more appealing. This perfect lion is called Joseph and you may recognise him from the MGM trailer at the start of your favourite movie. I filmed him in Los Angeles for an advertising campaign. Joseph always looks his best, the morning that I met him his mane had been freshly blow-dried and he'd eaten a fine breakfast of prime steak.

The difference between the two pictures is the look in the lions' eye. The wild one has a look of survival, of not knowing where the next meal is coming from. The look in Joseph's eye is different, he knows where the next meal is coming from and his only worry is whether it will be steak or chicken.

The Lion is widespread in Africa south of the Sahara and is plentiful in wildlife parks

African Lions are perhaps the most well known of all big cats, mainly due to their easy accessibility and the predominance of TV series featuring them. Male lions weigh in excess of 190 kg and stand 1.2 metres at the shoulder. Lions live in groups called prides, which may number up to thirty animals. The prides are run by the females and not as popularly believed, by the males. The males job is simple – they provide security for the pride from other males and defend any kills against other predators such as hyenas.

It was early one June morning when I came the closest to dying for my art. I wanted to get an extreme picture of a lioness stalking through the grass, but instead of strapping the camera to the front of the jeep I actually wanted to be there to take it. My guide Gavin, always willing to challenge me to the limit of my courage, showed me how by walking up to a lioness with a blanket on his head. Believe it or not lions run away from humans because they are scared of us, so the blanket was used to mask our human shape. I remember well the moment that Gavin came back to the jeep, handed me the blanket and uttered those immortal words – "your go". Nervously I donned my blanket, grabbed my camera, and began to slowly move away from the vehicle towards the lioness sitting in the grass. As I crept closer she stood up, turned and started to walk away. Now, I'm used to women doing this to me in discos the world over, and I was happy to have shown my bravado/stupidity to my guide.

I backed off slowly (you never show your back to a cat as it will jump on it by instinct), and was just relaxing when the lioness turned and stared at me intently. She then crouched low and began to stalk me, all I could see through the lens were her inquisitive eyes focused intently into mine and all I could hear was the sound of her moving through the grass towards me...

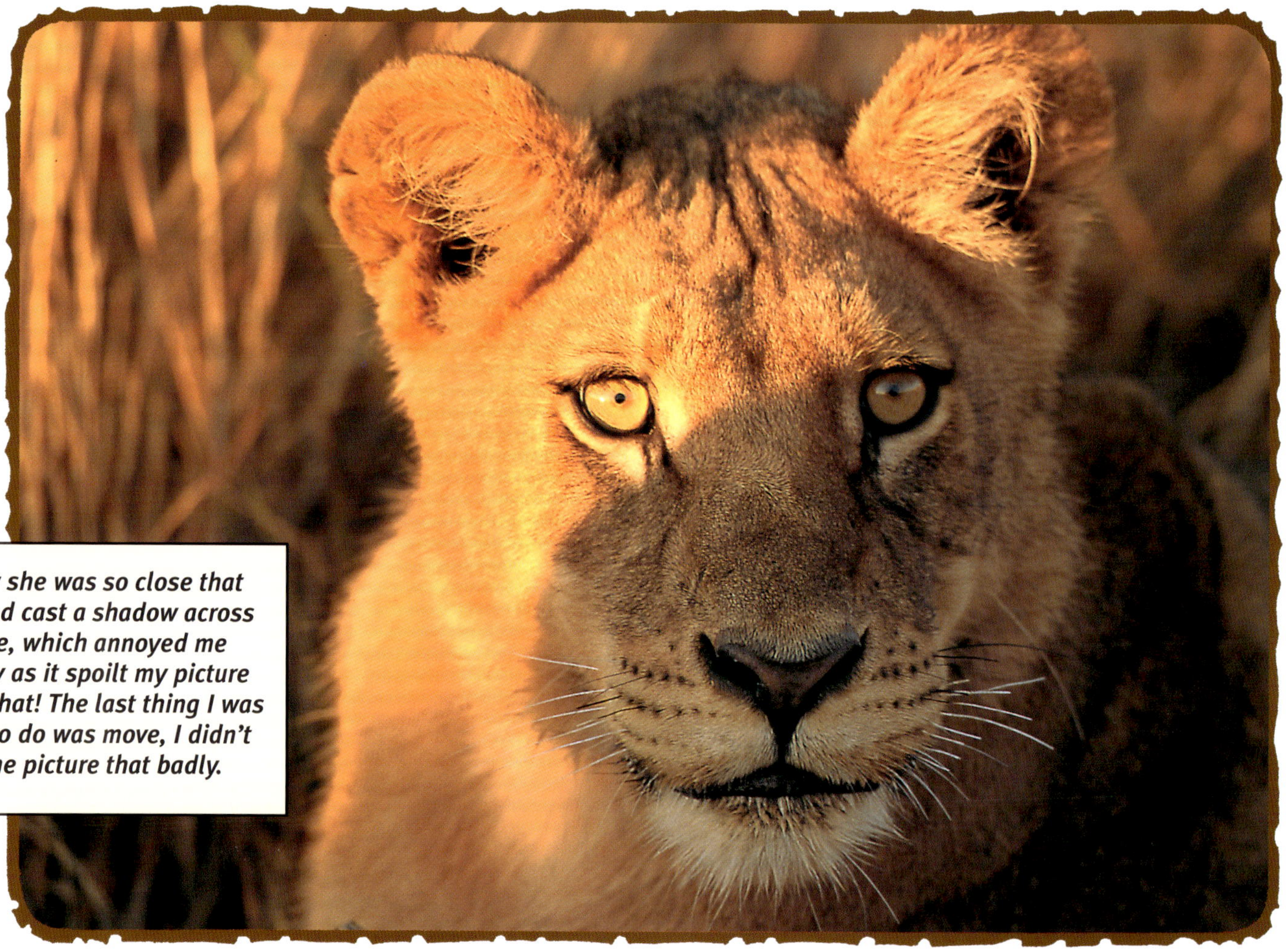

By now she was so close that my head cast a shadow across her face, which annoyed me slightly as it spoilt my picture somewhat! The last thing I was going to do was move, I didn't want the picture that badly.

EYE TO EYE

"Sit down and stay still" Gavin hissed from the truck and I nervously obliged. She continued to stare at me and I knew that one mistake could be my last. I'd been close to Grizzly Bears before and knew that I had to avoid eye contact, which sounds easy to do on paper but when you are faced with a lioness staring at you it's difficult not to look at her. I did toy with the idea of giving her the blanket to deal with, but the look in her eye quickly convinced me that it was me she was interested in.

By now she was so close that the low sun cast a shadow across her face, with horror I realised that it was my head that was causing the shadow. I gulped, then twice again for good measure, and tried to concentrate on taking the picture. Then, just as I thought things couldn't possibly get worse, I heard the unmistakable sound of crunching bone. I turned slowly and saw that one of her sisters was happily chewing on the remains of the last photographer to try this, I hoped she didn't like the taste.

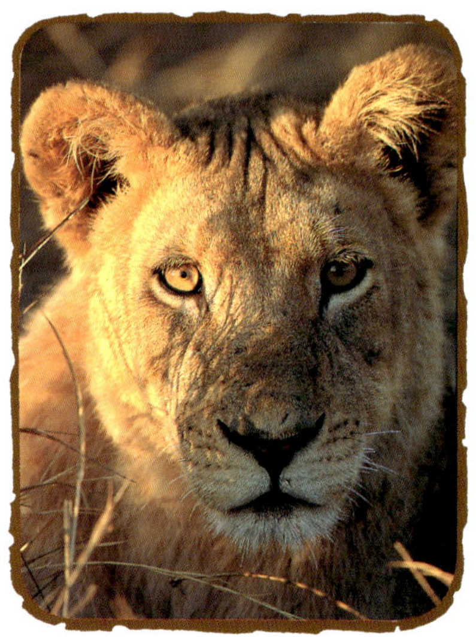

We sat there in silence for several minutes, she stared at me intently whilst I tried to do nothing which would make her even more inquisitive.

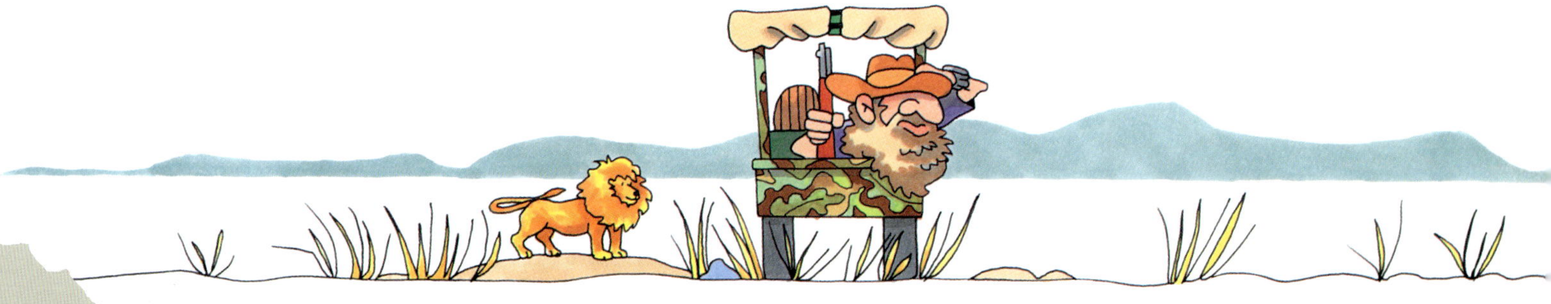

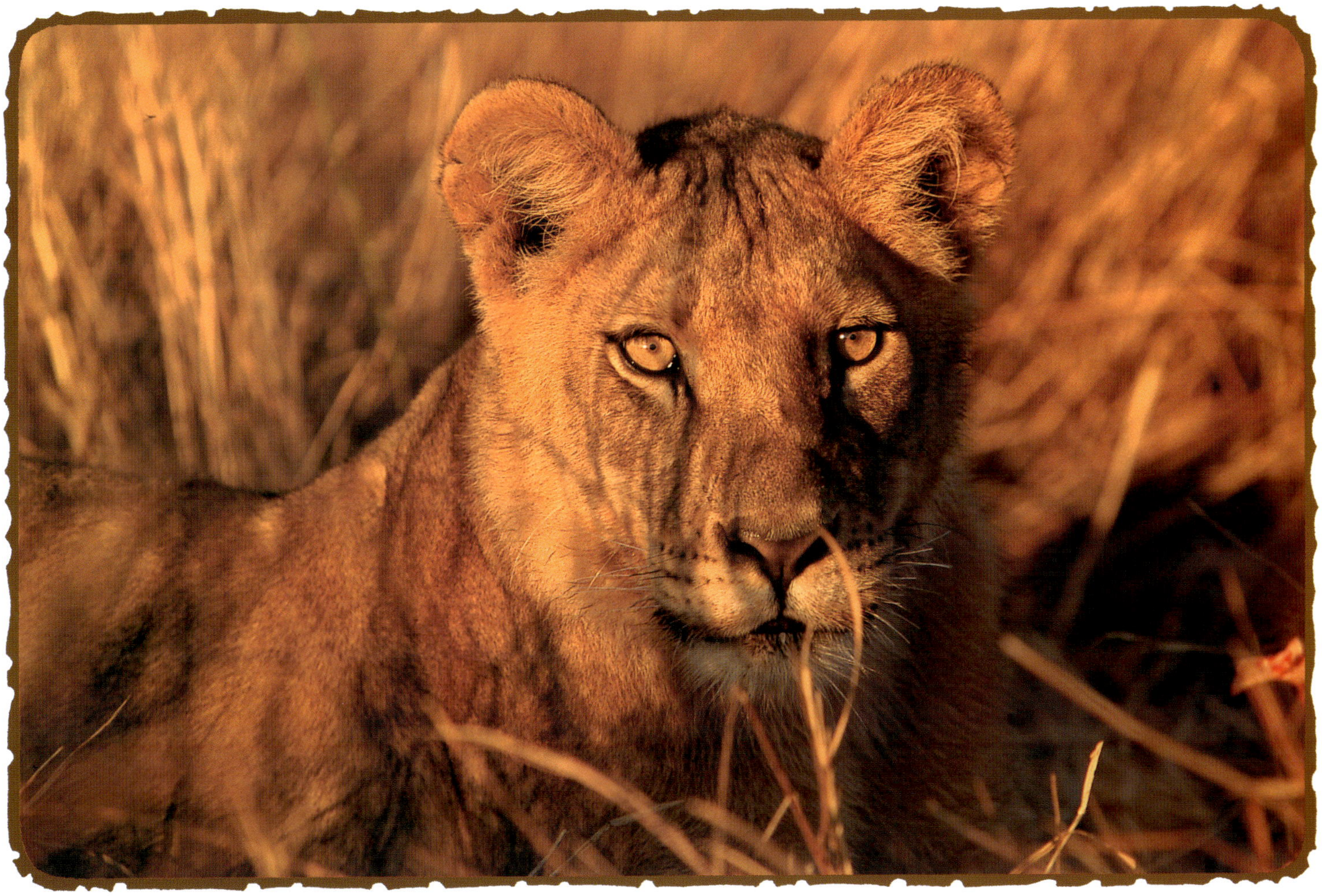

Lions eat a wide variety of prey which doesn't usually include wildlife photographers. They favour Wildebeest (they are so stupid even I could get one), Impala and Zebra but are great opportunists and will take anything that happens to walk by on two or four legs including giraffes, buffalo, birds, turtles and even fish. I once saw two lions happily chasing an Ostrich, which is a sight in itself!

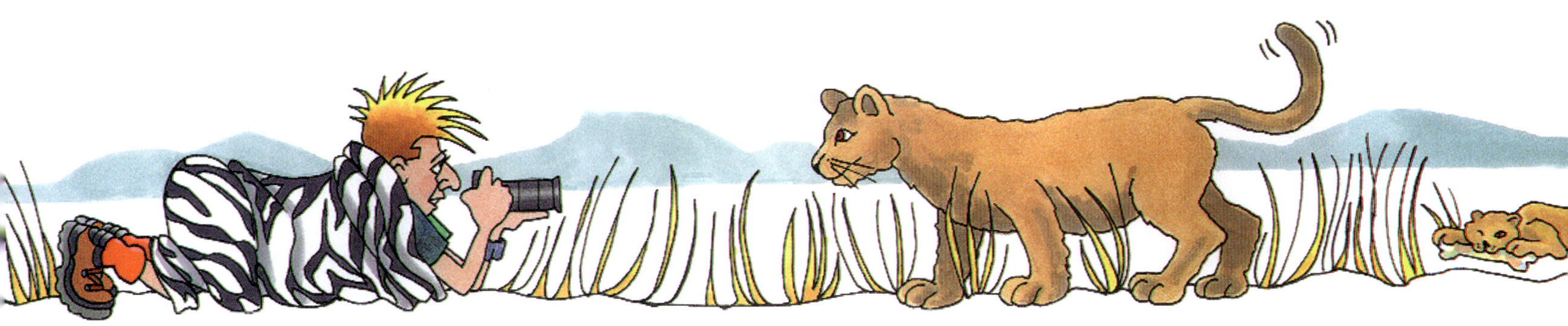

My musings were interrupted by the sound of the jeep's engine starting up, this galvanised the lioness into action but fortunately she moved away in the opposite direction from me. The jeep arrived and my guide hauled me in, "You're lucky" he said, pointing to the other side of the jeep. A fully grown male lion was watching us, his beautiful long mane blowing gently in the breeze. He'd appeared from nowhere, if he'd have seen me in the grass then I would have been dead, stone cold dead, luckily the truck shielded his view. I tried to be positive about it, thinking that at least then I would have got a follow-up to my king of the beasts picture on the opening pages. This time however it would have been from underneath the lion, with its jaws closing around my camera. Would I do it again?... Absolutely.

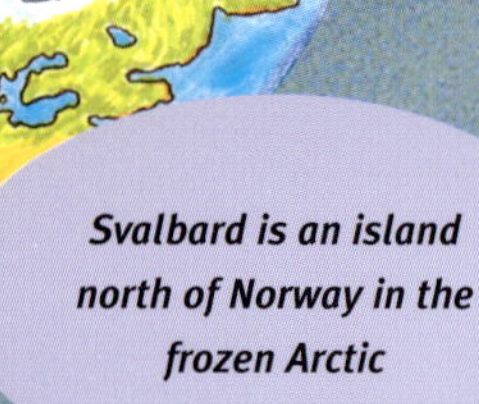

LORDS of the ARCTIC

My first impression of Svalbard came just after my flight from the mainland had landed, when my fellow passengers began to undertake a remarkable transformation. Trainers were replaced by large fur-lined boots, bulky down jackets took the place of anoraks and Balaclavas became the fashion accessory to wear.
I felt very out of place in my jeans and fleece. The airline pilot gave the usual welcome message, *"Welcome to Spitsbergen, the local time is 4:30 in the morning and it's... -25 degrees"*. My god, WHAT DID HE SAY?
The outside door was opened and an icy blast swept through the plane, chilling parts that shouldn't really be chilled and welcoming me to Svalbard.

Svalbard is a wonderful place for polar bears. Surrounded by pack ice for 8 months of the year, it provides them with the perfect habitat to do bear things like hunting seals, mating, courting and of course the most important facet of bear life, sleeping. Svalbard is a challenging and dangerous place, it's bad enough trying to stay alive with so many bears around, but we also had to deal with the cold, arctic storms that appear from nowhere and temperamental beasts called snowmobiles.

On Svalbard you are out on your own, and I rely totally on the skill and experience of my guide, Arne Kristoffersen, to keep me alive. Svalbard for me is a truly special place I hope you'll agree after reading my adventures in the following pages. Polar Bears are truly the Lords of the Arctic, lets go north to meet them.

The polar bear is found in all of the polar regions of the northern hemisphere which includes Russia, Norway, Greenland, the United States and Canada. The population is pretty healthy, it is estimated that there are currently somewhere between 20,000 and 40,000 polar bears with Canada's population of 15,000 bears being the largest group. The polar bear's scientific name, Ursus maritimus, means Sea Bear and they are primarily found in coastal areas, where the movement of sea ice creates perfect conditions for their favourite food – seals.

Just when you think it's safe to stop and have lunch, two bears peer at you from over an iceberg!

Polar Bears are full of surprises, sometimes they are even pleasant! We'd followed two sets of footprints for over an hour when suddenly two heads popped over the top of a ridge in front of us. Mothers with cubs normally head for the horizon when they see a snowmobile, but for once the wind was in our favour and we were dressed in white camouflage clothing. They came ambling towards us, the inquisitive cub running in front of the mother. It stopped on top of a ridge and drew itself up on its hind legs to try to peek over the top of the snowmobiles at us crouching behind.

The contrast between the needs of my photography and the needs for our survival were made very evident to me after I'd photographed this stunning iceberg. Arne marked its position on his snowmobile's GPS and the next day we returned with ice axes to hack huge pieces off it. No, we weren't creating modern art, but replenishing our water supply. Snow is not very good as a water supply, it contains impurities and you have to dig a few shovel loads to get even a saucepan full of water. Ice is much better and a small hand sized piece would give us enough water to cook dinner and make up our coffee flasks for the next few days.

CLOSE ENCOUNTER

It had been a long, frustrating day out on the ice searching for bears. We had found several, but whenever we approached they decided that Russia was a more attractive option, and headed at speed for the horizon. Svalbard is an expensive place to be and I imagined my bank manager demonically removing my overdraft facility, gleefully cutting all my cards in half and dancing naked on my burning cheque books if I came back with no pictures. With such thoughts to spur me on I stopped the snowmobile by a beautiful clear iceberg.

It was a stunning blue from one side, and from the other the setting sun viewed through it was a mass of shimmering gold. I walked around looking for the best angle, whilst Arne broke out the coffee.

After several minutes I was happily clicking away when Arne came up behind me and whispered "Andy, you're being watched by a polar bear". Well I've had things said to me in the past that caused a reaction – "Andy, you've passed your degree" *(through an alcohol-induced blur)*, "Andy, here's a pay-rise" *(from a horizontal position on the floor)* but this really got my attention.

For a moment I thought the bear had lost interest, then it strode up on top of the ridge and looked down on us...

CLOSE ENCOUNTER

I looked and sure enough a cream-coloured head with two beady black eyes was staring at us round the corner of a nearby iceberg. I like to think that it stared more at Arne than me as he has more meat on his bones, and I seriously considered running. This was a bad idea, not because I'm a slow runner *(I only have to run faster than Arne when you think about it)* but for the simple fact that it would invite a chase. So quietly we set off towards the snowmobiles; funny but they suddenly seemed an awful lot further away than I remembered leaving them. The polar bear followed us, Oh great.

We reached the relative safety of the snowmobiles, which were parked under a small ridge. Keeping one eye on the ridge, I turned to speak to Arne and found him putting bullets into a particularly nasty looking Clint Eastwood style Magnum 44. Come to think of it he does look a little like Clint in the right light. Polar bears are incredibly dangerous, unpredictable animals and to be in their environment without protection would be suicide. The guns however, were just there as deterrents and I knew that Arne would only use them to scare the bear into dropping me from its jaws. Just as I was thinking these delightfully positive thoughts, the polar bear strode up the ridge in front of us. Mr. Absolutely Wetting his Pants invaded my body but Mr. Cool photographer fought a valid rear guard action and managed to get some pictures for me. A polar bear, the largest land carnivore in the world, was now standing a mere 10 metres away, the time for jokes was over.

Polar Bears are great roamers and spend most of their time wandering the sea-ice in search of an unsuspecting seal. It has been estimated that an individual polar bear may potentially cover an area of 100,000 square miles during its lifetime. Of course bears, being bears, are inherently lazy and if they find a great seal hangout with females to mate with then they will stay in the area for life.

The polar bear sat down on the ridge and watched us. I couldn't have asked for a more perfect scene, surrounded by blue icebergs, a purple hue spreading across the sky, and an imposing polar bear sitting in the middle of it. The bear watched our every move – I was struggling to load film in the camera with hands so cold that they felt like claws, whilst Arne sat astride his snowmobile coolly waiting. The bear seemed perfectly at ease with us and I began to wonder why polar bears had such a fearsome reputation. This bear had a very soft feminine face, a flawless coat and a permanently quizzical look. You can hardly blame it for finding us so fascinating, I may not be the most interesting object to look at in the world, but anything is better than endless miles of ice.

As if it couldn't stand the tension any more, the bear stood up and strode purposefully down the ridge towards us. I hoped that my snowmobile would give me some kind of protection and a few seconds more life.

STAND OFF

After a tense 15 minute stand-off, the bear changed the stakes. Abruptly it stood up, stretched its massive body with a groan, and headed purposefully down the slope towards us. I squatted down behind my snowmobile, partly to give me a better angle but really to give Arne a clear shot if he needed it. We were 10 seconds and counting from being ex-humans and I prepared for the worst.

Arne, not wanting to become close friends with the bear, started the engine of his snowmobile and revved as hard as he could. This was quite an achievement as snowmobiles are notoriously temperamental when cold and I wouldn't bet any money on them starting for the first few minutes. Bears hate the sound of the engines and the smell of the exhaust fumes that come with it,

this one was thankfully no exception and ran back to the top of the ridge.

The bear stood and stared at us for several minutes, a confused look on its face. For all we knew, the bear might not have harboured any bad intentions towards us and just wanted to chew the leather on the snowmobile seats, something that they love doing. Discretion was the better part of valour as Polar Bears are the most dangerous and unpredictable land animal and we didn't want to take the chance of being dinner.

We decided to leave the bear to its thoughts and drove off into the hastening gloom. Polar Bears have been known to follow snowmobile tracks, ours led straight back to the hut and the tasty leather seats. I spent a restless night imagining every sound outside was our friend coming for a follow-up visit.

As Arne revved the snowmobile, the bear retreated to the top of the ridge and stared at us.

HOME SWEET HOME!

During our time on Svalbard we stayed in a tiny hut on the edge of the sea-ice. I regarded it as home, it offered some protection from the fierce winds and bone-chilling temperatures outside. Talking of the temperature, sometimes inside we could get it up to about 5°C, which when compared to outside meant we walked around in T-shirts. At other times, like during a storm, all the heat got sucked up the chimney and there was ice on the INSIDE of all the windows. On days like these I rarely left my sleeping bag.

Some evenings I would sit outside the hut, stare at the mountains opposite and wonder if life could get any better. One look at the hut reminded me of who was in charge round here, as there were claw marks up the door and on the window frames. The previous year our hut had been the subject of a polar bear raid and somehow, don't ask me how or why, the polar bear carried the wood burning stove out onto the ice. Quite where it expected to get the wood from is another question entirely.

I used to dream of washing, but as it involved stripping naked, going outside, covering myself in soap then attempting to wipe myself dry before important bits started dropping off my body; I just got used to smelling badly. Water was a precious commodity, so washing my hands meant involved covering them in washing up liquid and, you guessed it, plunging them deep into a nearby snowdrift. I am not macho by any means, give me some nice scented soap and running hot water and I'll hum away whilst washing my hands for hours.

Arne amazed me by his resourcefulness and creativity, here he is making a binocular case from seal-skin. He spent hours patiently stitching it together, ignoring the grumbling coming from deep within my sleeping bag.

As Arne did all the cooking, one of my chores was to do the washing up. Unlike normal home life when you find any excuse to leave the washing up till later, the chance of dipping your frozen hands into warm water was too much of a pleasure to miss.

If we weren't sleeping or cooking, the only reason to be inside the hut was to shelter from inclement weather. For me, these were the times of greatest frustration and boredom, and I'd usually spend the day grumbling away in my sleeping bag. I always take a little short-wave radio with me so I can listen to the BBC World Service, its amazing how the Archers can cheer you up on a dull day far from home. After being cooped up for days though, the radio was in serious danger of having a large knife stuck through it, especially if either of us heard the shipping forecast one more time. Arne would spend his time inside the hut either creating something useful or making sure his guns were ready for use. I was banned from using anything that fired ammunition, except when using the outside toilet when I was extremely vulnerable to a sneak polar bear attack. On my first day at the hut I tried out the thunderclap pistol on a target, and each time managed to land the thunderclap grenade behind it. In real life this would have exploded behind the polar bear and sent it running towards us, which was not the best idea.

Getting ready to go outside, unless you were desperate for the toilet, involved ten minutes of pulling on as many layers of wet, smelly clothing as you could. Arne's company, Svalbard Wildlife Service, provided me with an outer suit and a dog fur hat which kept me remarkably warm.
Dog fur is used because it is a superb insulator and dries very quickly when wet, not very trendy but who cares.

Arne had an amazing knack
of spotting polar bears and
figuring out the best way to
get to them through the
chunks of pack ice.

LOOKING FOR BEARS

When the weather allowed, our time would mostly be
spent cruising the pack ice looking for signs of bears.
At the start of the day we'd wrestle the snowmobiles high
up the snow cliffs on the coast to get a wide vista over
the ice below. I used to dread this as my control of the
snowmobile was poor to say the least; I invariably ended
up rolling it and having the indignity of Arne appearing
and having to help me out from underneath it.
Still, sacrifices have to be made for one's art. Once we'd
struggled to the top, Arne would scan the ice below for
signs of bears trudging around looking to create
mischief. We could see for miles and bears, believe it or
not, are very easy to spot because they stand out against
the ice. *"Uh, but surely they're white"* I hear you cry, well
they aren't white at all, but a creamy mayonnaise colour.
If we found one then we'd hurtle down the slope,
hanging on for dear life, and start to work our way
towards it. If we didn't find one then we'd cruise around
the ridges in the pack ice looking for footprints. Polar
Bears use the ridges to hunt for seals so we knew that
it was a good place to start.

Arne spotted this bear when it was
fast asleep in a small gully.
We parked the snowmobiles a long
way off to avoid waking it, and crept
closer until the bear suddenly raised
a sleepy head and sniffed at us.

I was bored. I'd thrown my knife a hundred times against an imaginary target of a traffic warden, slept enough for a year and was beginning to get severe cabin fever. Outside the hut, a storm had raged for three days, the wind rattling the windows and finding its way through the cracks in the wooden walls. We'd seen the storm coming the day before whilst out on the ice and raced it all the way home, aware that if it caught us we'd be stuck out on the ice until it blew over. If that happened we'd be vulnerable to the bears as we couldn't see them approaching, but worse, we'd be out in nightmare weather. Luckily we made it to the hut with minutes to spare, as the first winds battered our little wooden home.

When the wind finally quieted on the third day, Arne and I needed no encouragement to escape the confines of the hut. It was definitely a good idea as the hut was developing a special odour of its own. We gunned the snowmobiles into life, and headed out into the frozen bay area; the storm was still raging out on the ice but the wind had changed enough to give our bay some shelter.

Using the snowmobiles as a wind-break – I always knew those seaside holidays as a kid would come in useful – I squatted down low and set up my camera gear. It was then that I noticed the blood on the ice around the bear. As if on cue the bear stooped down and stood up with a seal in its mouth. We became very wary of the bear, animals will always protect their food, and this bear had gone to a lot of time and trouble to get its seal.

Polar Bears are amazing hunters and I've been fortunate to witness it several times. They first search the pack ice for indications that a seal has built a cave underneath it. The key to the hunt is the polar bear's hyper-sensitive nose, which has to be good enough to sniff out a seal cave 1-2 metres under the ice, from over a kilometre away. Believe me seals are smelly, even I could find one from a few metres away! I once watched as a Polar Bear covered a huge area of pack ice, its nose pressed firmly against the ground. Suddenly it stopped, pressed itself flat against the ice and inched forward on its belly. Seals are very aware of the hairy danger above and the slightest sound would give the polar bear away. Satisfied that the hole was directly underneath, the Polar Bear waited on all fours for a tell-tale noise below. After about eight hours of laying motionless, it suddenly started to raise itself into a strike position.

The bear raised itself to its full height and smashed both paws downwards breaking through the ice. Ideally it would block the cave exit with its head, but this time it failed and the seal managed to escape.

I felt the wind change on the side of my face. Felt is perhaps the wrong term as I'd lost the feeling through my three balaclavas *(including my high tech thermal propylene nitro-goretex di-ethyl toluene goat-lined one)* but I knew this could spell trouble. Sure enough, the wind now whipped though the bay, throwing up loose snow all around us, and making the bear impossible to see. When the swirling cleared I occasionally caught a glimpse of its creamy form staring intently at us, but conditions were becoming too borderline to carry on.

The last time we saw the bear it was headed for the shelter of the shore, dragging the seal carcass in its mouth. We started to head for home, the wind was blowing straight into our faces, taking our breath away and freezing it straight to our masks. The white cloud cover meant that it was impossible to make out any shapes ahead, and the ice looked like a flat white desert. I knew that it wasn't, and my fears were confirmed when Arne's snowmobile disappeared suddenly in front of me. I swerved to a stop to see him some 6-7 feet below, his snowmobile stuck at an angle to the sled he was towing. It took us an hour of digging to get the snowmobile out, during which I learnt some choice new Norwegian phrases and swapped him some good East London ones. We decided that when a polar bear has had enough of the weather it's time to leave, and we headed back to smell central.

I sat out on the face of the ice in the full blast of the Arctic wind whilst the polar bear dozed in the shelter of the iceberg.

THE ICEBERG BEAR

The storm finally relented after five days, the sun rising purposefully over the mountains behind us. By now the smell in the hut was unbearable, and we'd have gone out no matter how bad the weather was just to escape it. As usual, we took the snowmobiles up high to get a view across the ice. Nothing was moving down below, except for the ice, which appeared to be flowing like a river in front of us. Arne frowned, "There's a helluva wind storm down there, blowing only 2 foot high across the ice" he said. We looked at each other, got onto our snowmobiles and drove down onto the ice without a word. Anything was better than returning to the hut.

As soon as we got onto the ice the wind hit us, and my outermost balaclava instantly froze. We made for the direction of a huge iceberg to try to get some shelter, but we'd been beaten to it. For there in the shelter of the iceberg, was a sleeping polar bear. We took the snowmobiles in slowly so that we didn't wake the bear; I'm grumpy enough in the mornings, and this bear has more teeth than me and a much stronger desire to use them. The wind, for once, was in our favour and was so strong that it blew both our exhaust fumes and the sound of the engines well away from the bear. We stopped some 200 metres from the iceberg, and I set up my gear.

The bear had the right idea, totally sheltered from the wind and riding out the storm. We on the other hand were totally exposed and getting colder by the minute. I tried to ignore the cold but it became exceedingly difficult to work; Arne's console thermometer gave the temperature as -35°C, and with the wind chill it was around -50°C. My hands confirmed this by freezing completely, and I resorted to changing film using a combination of teeth and wrists. By now my hands were frozen solid and the gloves weren't warming them up – if they stayed colder for much longer there would be a real danger of frostbite which would ruin my tennis serve. Arne, hero as always, saved the day by baring his armpits and shoving my hands between them. Now, after ten days of not washing and some very sweaty snowmobile work that doesn't sound like a very pleasant thing to do, and normally I would have complained loudly, but this was an extreme case and I was grateful. He just smiled back at me.

Once we'd found the bear sheltering in the iceberg, the next problem was how to take its picture to show off the beauty of the scene. With my monster lens I could zoom right into its eyeball, but that wouldn't have recorded anything about the sheer beauty that I could see. So I opted for a slightly wider outlook, and you can see the result on the following pages.

Unlike wildlife photographers, polar bears are well adapted to the cold. Their first line of defence is the thick winter coat, which consists of two layers; an outer coat of long, glossy guard hairs and dense white underfur. These guard hairs are translucent which transmit the sun's heat down to the polar bear's skin, which is black. The combination of the black skin and the thick layers of fat underneath it, make sure that heat loss is kept to a minimum.

The bear slept on through all this activity, and my hands started returning to life. To keep us warm Arne suggested a bout of wrestling, and I'm sorry to say that Norway won hands down.
To an onlooker it would have looked ridiculous, two grown men dressed as astronauts rolling around in a snow-storm with the world's most dangerous land predator asleep within striking range of them. To the bear it would have seemed strange as well, but it was still comatose and completely unaware of the drama in front of it.

After only an hour we were both frozen solid and kicked the snowmobiles into life to go home. The bear raised a sleepy head in our direction to see what all the noise was about, then promptly put it down again and went straight back to sleep. I smiled to myself whilst trying to drive my snowmobile with two claws for hands, it was undoubtedly the coldest experience of my life.

A BIG MALE APPROACHES

I think that my most treasured memory from Svalbard was a courtship that I witnessed from start to finish. No it wasn't my chat-up attempts in the local bar, but rather a rarely-seen encounter between two polar bears. It had everything a good story should: a fight between two rivals, a tender love scene and a happy ending. All of it played out in bearovision around our snowmobiles. It started when we found two sets of footprints heading towards a group of icebergs. We were about to follow them when a speck of mayonnaise on the horizon caught my attention. I wiped my glasses but it was still there. It was a polar bear, a very long way off. We waited, and soon it was close enough to make out as a big male, a very big male, and it was headed directly for us.

Camera in hand, I crawled out from the safety of the snowmobiles and laid down flat on the ice to get an ant's eye view of the rapidly approaching bear. Arne smiled and said laconically *"You do realise that you look like a seal out there dressed in black"*. For one awful moment I thought the bear agreed, fortunately when he was about 15 metres away he moved off to one side.

The big male bear soon picked up the trail of fresh footprints that we'd first found. He had just started following them when a head appeared round the iceberg in front of him. It was another polar bear. He took one look at the big guy and decided that retreat was the safest option. After a few hundred metres he stopped

and turned to face the other bear, and I suspected we
were about to witness a real polar bear fight.
I'd expected a good bit of mauling, or at least some left
hooks, but in fact all they did was growl at each other.
Or to be more precise, the big guy growled at the smaller
one, who backed off. Having been in that situation myself
I agreed that backing off was a good idea. Polar bears
this size can injure each other severely in a physical
contest, and in this environment injuries can quickly lead
to death. So, they avoid physical contact and instead rely
on size and threat to do the talking. The smaller guy
decided that he wanted to live to be a big guy one day,
and headed for the coast at a gallop, nervously looking
back over his shoulder. The big guy didn't follow
because, as we were soon to find out, he had something
far more important in mind.

Polar Bears grow very large, very very large; in fact they are the largest land carnivore. Adult polar bears stand approximately 1 metre ($3^1/_2$ feet) tall when on all fours and have an approximate body length from nose to tail of 250 to 350 centimetres ($8 ^1/_4$ to $11^1/_2$ feet). Females typically weigh in the area of 300 kilograms (660 pounds). Males are generally larger and usually weigh 500 to 600 kilograms (1100 to 1320 pounds). They can grow much larger, there is a record of an adult male polar bear weighing over 1000 kilograms (2200 pounds). The polar bear that you see in this picture was a really well developed adult male, probably around 600 kg in weight, as he walked the ice crushed beneath him.

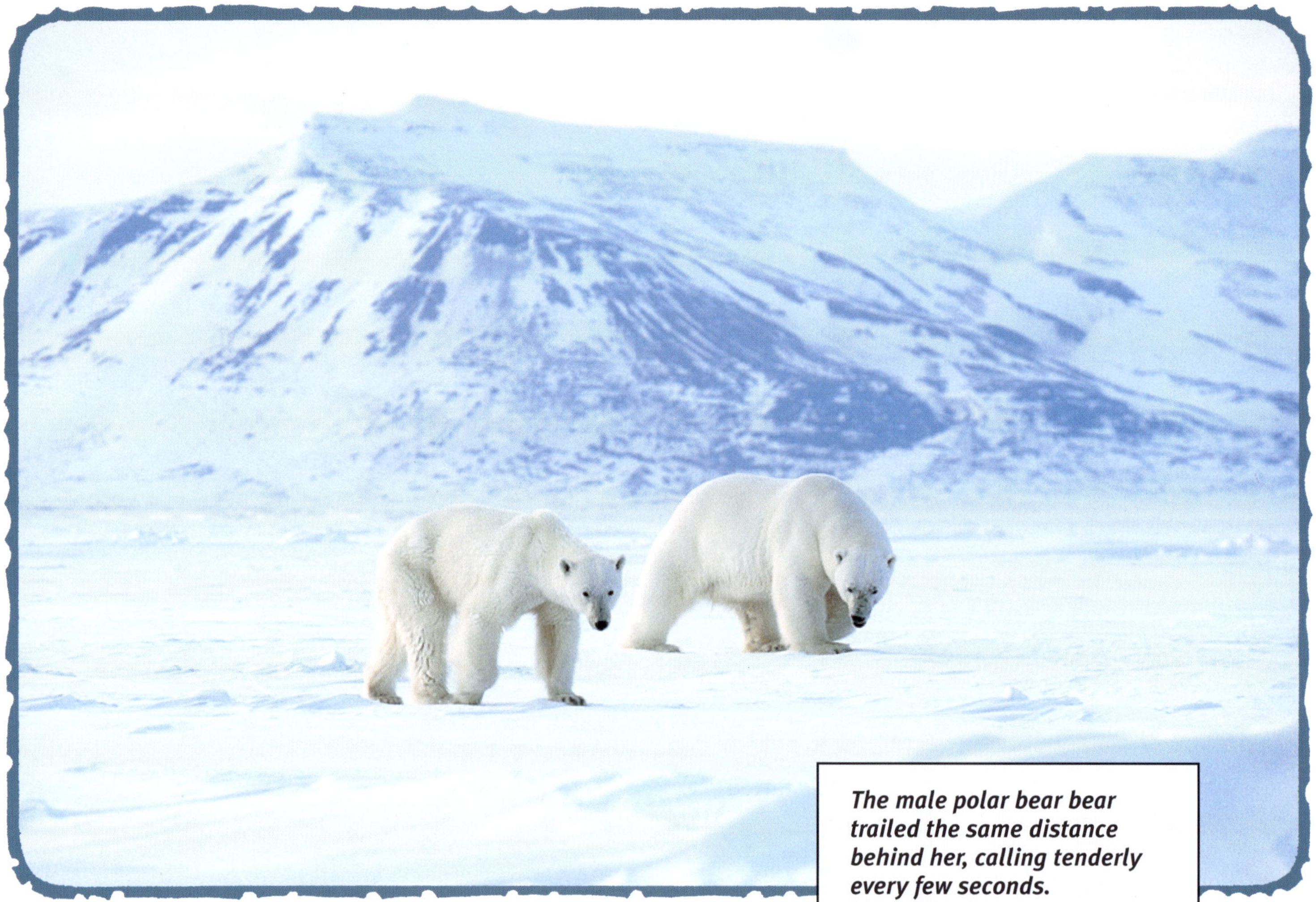

The male polar bear bear trailed the same distance behind her, calling tenderly every few seconds. This behaviour continued on and off for twelve hours or so, time has little meaning as from April, Spitsbergen has twenty-four hours of daylight.

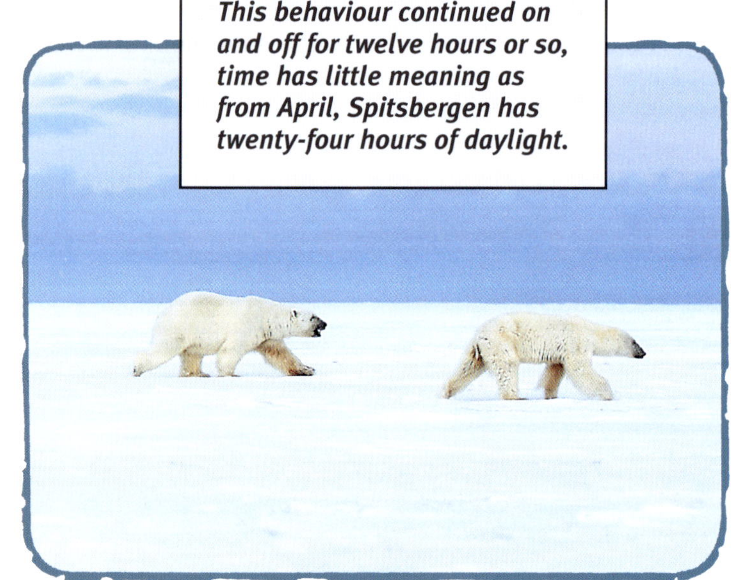

THE COURTSHIP BEGINS

The bear disappeared behind the iceberg and after a few minutes re-appeared on the other side. At least I thought it was him, but when I looked closer I realised it was a much smaller bear, a female. The big guy had fought for the oldest reason in the world, over a woman. She didn't seem so keen on him and, spying us, made a bee-line for our snowmobiles. She didn't run, just plodded along in the way that polar bears do, but with every step she brought the big guy closer to us. He fixed us with a stare that spoke volumes. Arne and I looked at each other and immediately started packing the gear back into the snowmobiles, the smelly hut infinitely more attractive than a large lovesick polar bear. Abruptly she stopped her advance, our movements disconcerting her, and then started to walk slowly around us. He followed her; now I knew what it felt like to be in a wagon train with the injuns charging round the outside.

For once the wind had dropped and all around was silence. It was broken by a gentle "mewing" sound, and I realised that the male bear was calling tenderly to the female. This was obviously part of the courtship, and she made the most of it by trailing him round us for three hours. Diligently he followed her, calling all the time, its was truly beautiful scene as they walked in front of the mountains.

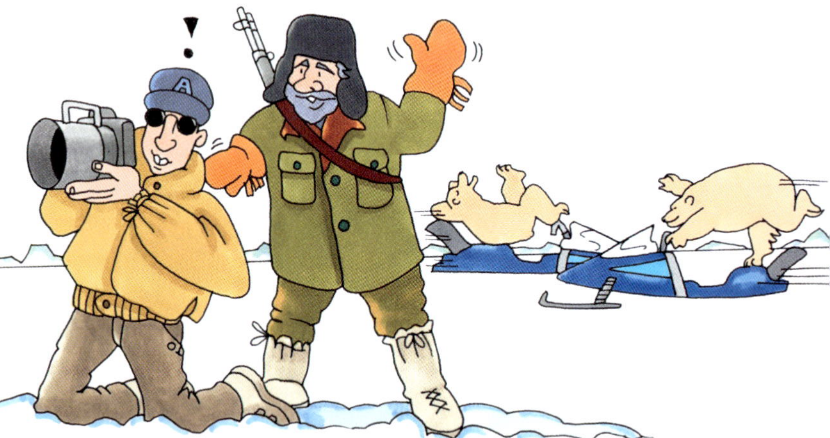

The female stopped near a pack ice ridge and started staring intently at the ice. *"She's hunting seals"* muttered Arne. The big guy settled down next to her for a free lunch, it was clearly going to be a long wait. We decided to alternate the watch, one of us on guard whilst the other tried to sleep on the snowmobile. It was my turn first, and god only knows how I managed to fall asleep but sleep I did, that is until Arne shook me awake. I noticed that the sun was noticeably lower and the polar bears had vanished from their earlier position. Arne pointed them out to me, behind us and heading out onto the ice.

It was the moment we'd been waiting for, she turned and accepted him for the first time, after days of patient effort on his part.

THE COURTSHIP HOTS UP

Finally, and we breathed a sigh of relief on his behalf, she turned and let him catch her up. He was huge next to her, probably three times her weight, but he never made any aggressive moves. He just kept tenderly calling as he approached her, head bowed low *(I bet you are loving this ladies aren' t you)*, until they touched. It was a special moment, she'd finally accepted his advances and I almost felt a tear in my eye. Well I would have done except it would have been a lump of ice. The voyeur in me wanted them to get down to some serious business, but no, they simply went back to the same routine of follow the leader.

We'd been out now for well over 18 hours and decided to retreat back to the hut to get some supplies, as we didn't want to miss the later stages of the courtship. Its always important to eat regularly in the cold as your body needs fuel to survive. Arne marked the position with his GPS and we set off back to smelly towers.

After a shower, five-course meal and a G&T *(ermm I don' t think so)*, we returned to find both of them sound asleep, together. Now, I want to know what went on in those few hours we were away. We waited and waited but they showed no inclination to let us into their secret.

The two bears slept for hours, clearly something had made them tired but we could only speculate what. It would have been a great picture for me to get, a unique shot of two polar bears mating, but alas it was not to be.

SLEEPING BEARS

Time passed, and eventually Arne said *"Andy, it's time to go"*. We had a one hundred and twenty mile snowmobile ride back to town to catch my plane home, and as the flight only leaves once a week it was vital that I didn't miss it. I wanted to find any excuse to stay but knew that Arne was right. Sadly I drove slowly away, looking over my shoulder at the bears until the headland finally blocked my view. They'd shared an intimate experience with us, something that I will remember for the rest of my life. As we climbed the coast back to the hut I looked back and could just make out the pair of them, heading out on the sea ice towards who knows what. In a few days they would part, probably never to meet again, but it's my ambition to return and photograph the next stage in the female's life, when her cubs emerge from their den for the first time...

An EXPEDITION to JAPAN

Japan, home of Sushi bars and Casio watches, is a land of extreme contrasts. Driving around the high tech neon architecture of Tokyo, you'd be forgiven for wondering if there was any wildlife at all in Japan, but less than three hours drive away lies the breathtaking snow-capped natural splendour of Mount Fuji, which dominates the scenery for miles around.

Japanese culture takes its influence from many of the native species found on the islands, notably the Japanese Crane and the Snow Monkey. I loved my trip to Japan, it is a spectacular place, with wildlife that exhibits a grace and beauty that I have rarely seen anywhere else. And the Sushi is good too!

Mount Fuji is the world's greatest photospot. When we arrived early in the morning, in time to catch the sunrise, we were greeted by rows of tripods staked out on the ridge. The Japanese love their photography and they'd all reserved the prime spots in advance. it makes a change from beach towels I suppose. Anyway, the sunrise was beautiful over the mountain, the first rays of the sun sent a purple hue dancing across the upper slopes. The legions of photographers soon left so we just sat and enjoyed the peace before returning to the bustle of Tokyo.

Much of my time in Japan was spent on the northern island of Hokkaido. It's a magical place in winter, snow hangs delicately in the trees and ice floats in large floes off the coast.

The Crane raised its elegant head, opened its beak and I waited expectantly for its "trumpeting". The sound that came out was hardly orchestral, more like a throttled squawk, but to Japanese culture it's music. The Crane stands for many positive things in the Japanese culture; Cranes mate for life which shows fidelity, unlike most species the male shares the duties of raising the youngsters which demonstrates the power of a good marriage and their dancing shows happiness.

Every morning the Cranes took off from their overnight roost and headed for breakfast at a local feeding site. My guide, David Pike, stood on the far side of the field with a walkie-talkie, giving me warning when anything crane-like flew in our general direction.

DANCING CRANES

The story of the Crane hasn't always been a happy one. After a hunting ban was lifted in the 19th century they were hunted so heavily that for many years they were believed to be extinct. Then, a small group were found breeding in the middle of remote marshland, and the conservation story began. The Cranes reclaimed their protected status and their numbers slowly began to increase. The winters in their Hokkaido homelands are harsh and as Cranes are ground feeders, the covering of snow makes food very difficult to find. During a particularly harsh winter, help came from the local villagers who started an unofficial feeding program for. Realising the villagers had the right idea, the government established regular feeding sites for them, which have now become prime photospots.

We visited one of the Crane feeding grounds on a Saturday and it was absolute chaos; photographers were everywhere and all available space was taken up by camera gear. Japanese people are so friendly that space magically appeared for us. We were so much the centre of attention that I was interviewed by a local TV crew and filmed eating sushi!

When my guide David told me that Cranes danced, I had visions of a couple of wing flaps followed by the odd trumpet. When it started I stood there open-mouthed; I'd expected one crane to dance, maybe two at a push, but not a whole group. But dance they did, not the usual Andy Rouse effort of flailing limbs and failing footwork, but a graceful aerial ballet. Moreover the dancing was directed at the same partner all the time, their life partner.

The dance usually started with some posturing on the ground, with the wings outstretched and a strangely comical expression on the face. Then both partners would leap into the air, sometimes as high as 10ft, and pirouette. The cranes seemed to float on air, their huge outstretched wings acting like a parachute. I actually think they do it for sheer enjoyment!

I witness many things in my job, some of them legal, but often the tender moments between a mother and a baby animal are the most special.

SNOW MONKEYS

Snow Monkeys are incredibly cute *(young ones look like an alien with a blow dry)* and on my first morning I was lucky enough to spend several hours with a mother and her young baby. When we were first introduced, like any blind date, we were both nervous. The mother gave me a piercing look and showed me her long teeth, just in case I was in any doubt who was boss. The baby regarded me with an inquisitive look which convinced its mother to tolerate me; this probably saved me the pleasure of having her teeth planted in my backside.

After a while the mother and baby moved up the snow ridge and started to feed at the tree-line. I put on my trendy white arctic boots, did a michael jackson twirl for good measure, and followed them to the top. I was freezing cold after 30 minutes of crawling through the snow to approach them, worryingly so for some of my extremities. By now the baby had climbed an impossibly thin branch to get some choice tree buds, and studied me from above. I like to think it wasn't looking at my bald patch but it did seem to have a permanent smirk on its face.

The Snow Monkeys of this troop had a particular desire to spend their time in a warm bath. Nothing strange about this, I love nothing better than a foaming bath where I can sing all my favourite songs, but monkeys are not known for their tolerance to water (or my singing). The local area had many natural geothermal pools, but to save the tourists a long trek, the local authorities had sculpted one near the feeding centre. The monkeys loved it and would happily sit in it for hours, picking up food from the bottom, grooming or sleeping. I guess with the cold weather outside you could hardly blame them!

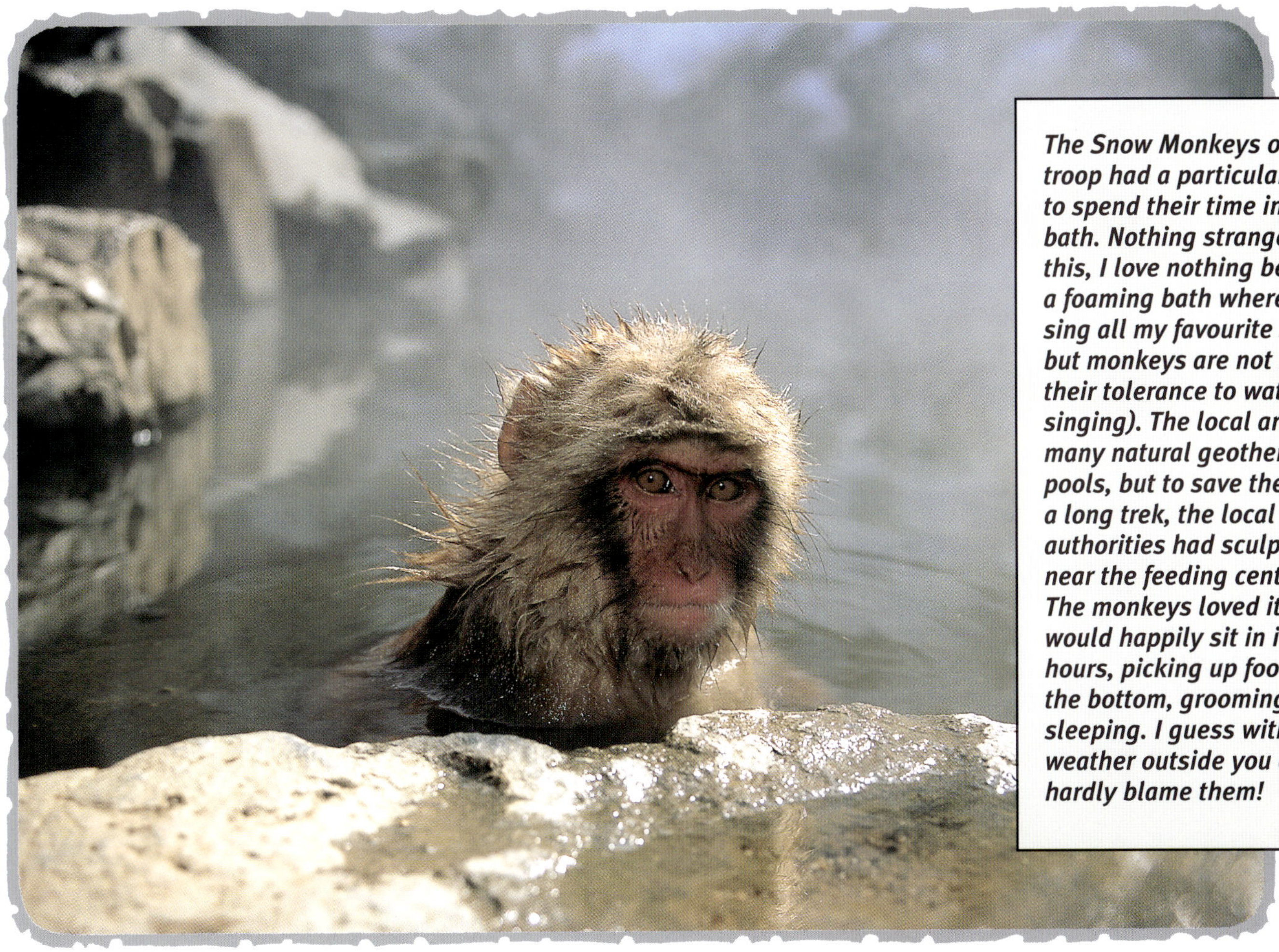

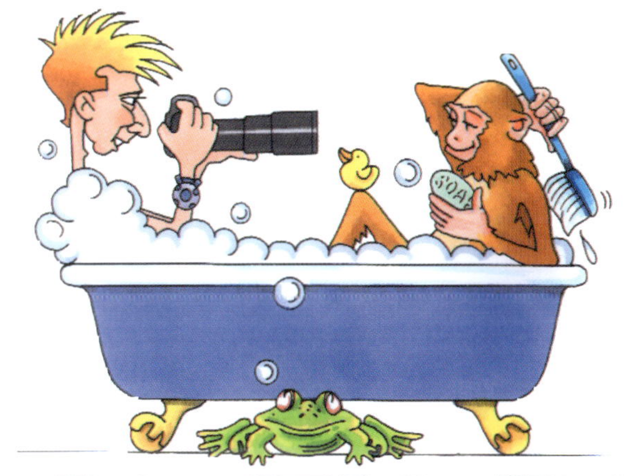

The Japanese Macaque, or Snow Monkey, lives farther north than any primate, except man. They have been very important to Japanese culture for many years and references to them appear in many ancient texts and drawings. Nowadays they are revered and there is even a special Monkey Temple to pay homage to their spirits. Snow Monkeys live in the high forests of Japan, in troops of up 30 animals. Like most animal societies, the females are in control of the troop, although a dominant male is allowed to think he's in control.

The only problem with the little darlings was their inquisitiveness. They loved to climb on my tripod, maliciously pull various useful parts off it and retreat to the hills before I could stop them.

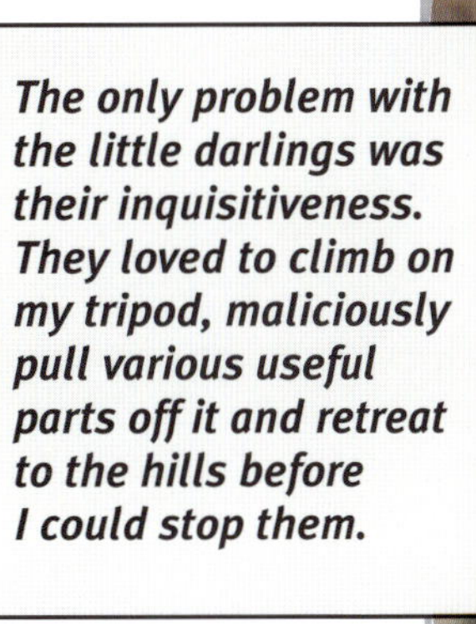

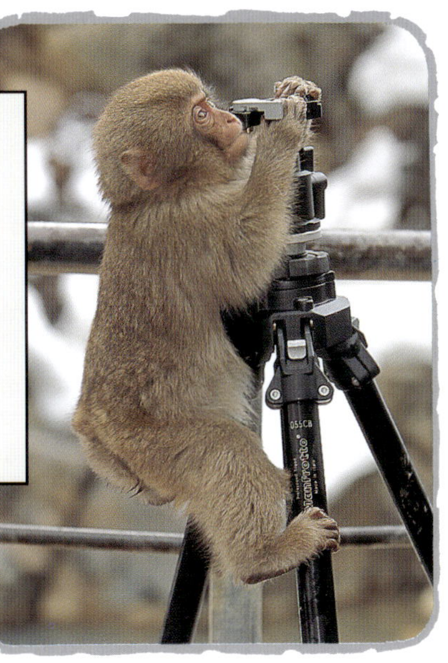

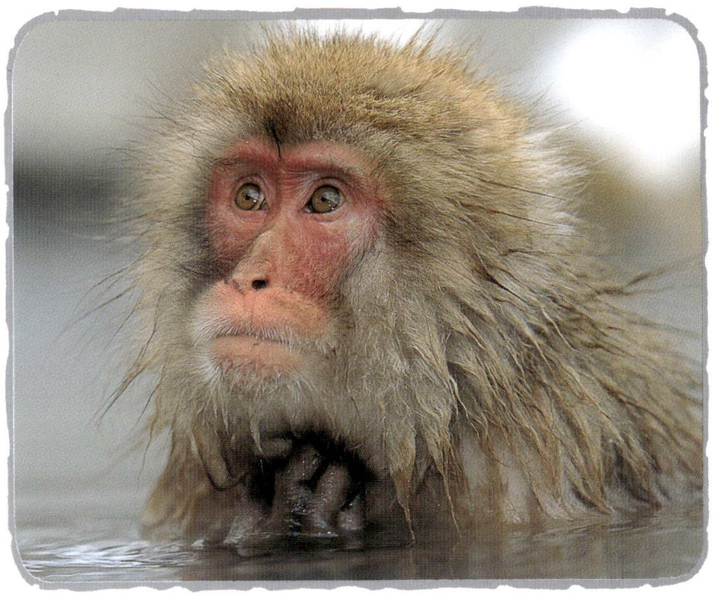

It was a beautiful sight to see the eagles sitting on the icebergs waiting for the sun to rise.

STELLER SEA EAGLES

I've always loved messing around in boats, undoubtedly the smelliest and most dangerous aquatic experience I've ever had came when photographing Steller Sea Eagles off the Hokkaido coast.

To get to them we hired a lunatic. His real job was as a boat captain, but he'd perfected the art of terrifying his passengers. We'd set off from harbour before dawn, wrapped up like eskimos as the temperature was around -15°C, and headed out towards the ice. The captain would spot a group of Stellers minding their own business on the ice floes and turn the boat towards them. Great, that's what we paid him for, the problem was there was usually a lot of ice between us and the eagles. Oh no, this was no problem to the captain, he'd just ram the ice floes with the boat to push them apart. He did this with such alarming regularity that I did seriously wonder if he had a full set of marbles; history has hardly been kind to boats that ram icebergs and I wondered if he'd ever seen the film Titanic.

As if the threat of icebergs wasn't enough, the assault on my nostrils was almost overpowering. We had crates and crates of fish stacked at the back of the boat, and the wind always seemed to blow the smell in my direction. The fish were used to attract the eagles, at some point a deckhand would jump onto a flat iceberg and empty them onto it. This was great for the eagles, but not so great for those of us who stood by the crates all the time and went home with the smell firmly attached to our clothes.

If the weather was bad then the eagles would stay in their roosts along the coastline.

During the winter the Nemuro Straits freeze and the eagles use the ice floes as mobile fishing perches. Life for them during these winter months is harsh, the climate in this part of Japan is very changeable and the area is prone to blizzards and fierce winds. The winds control the position of the ice floes, sometimes they are right against the shore whilst at other times they are many miles away. The eagles survive through all this inclement weather, and ramming raids by tourist boat captains, to breed in the summer months on the Kamchatka peninsula in Russia. Of all the wonderful sights that I saw on Hokkaido, the Steller Sea Eagle is the one that made the greatest impression on me, and the one that I can't wait to return to next year. The Sushi was also very good there!

The Red Fox is spread over most of Europe and Northern Asia. The North American Red Fox is similar.

The RED FOX

Those of you who have read this book from the start will probably have the impression that I'm a jet set wildlife photographer; my friend Lucy says that I have a champagne lifestyle on a lemonade budget which is a lot closer to the truth. If I had my choice I'd spend all my time on the South Downs of England photographing my beloved Roe Deer, Foxes, Badgers and Hares. It takes all my skill and cunning to get close to them, and unlike my expensive foreign trips, I can take all year recording every detail of their lives.

Of all the British mammals that I struggle to photograph, the Fox is my undoubted favourite. It's taken me years of watching, tracking, stalking and lurking in dark places to begin to understand them, and only now am I beginning to see the results on film. The problem with the fox is that all five senses are highly developed, with a sixth one added for knowing when I've got the camera with me. To get a photograph I have to outwit all these senses at the same time, if I give a single clue away then the fox will know I'm there.

Foxes are great survivors and have outwitted all man's attempts to eradicate them. They are generally solitary animals of the night, only coming together for mating or when rearing cubs. Foxes have long had a reputation for cunning, they can live under our noses and we'd never know they were about. The only clue to their presence is their smell, which I liken to two fat blokes playing squash for several hours in a closed room. I've read in many books that foxes bury food to come back for later, I have to take this opportunity to say that although I've seen my foxes burying food, I've never once seen any evidence that they remember where it is later!

I think its the beautiful coat that really attracts me to foxes, it seems to have an inner glow in any light.

To outwit their eyes and noses I wear trendy camouflage clothes that make me look like a walking oak tree; I'm not sure if it works as well as with deer but at least it gives the foxes a good laugh after a hard day on the farm. Foxes rely on their noses to give them the first indication of danger, so I have to make very sure that I smell like the forest.

This means that none of my clothes go anywhere near a washing machine and I never wear aftershave or deodorant the day I go tracking, both of which are unpopular at home but make me a favourite with the neighbourhood dogs.
To outwit the fox's perception of movement (its sixth sense if you like) I either sit under a piece of camouflage netting and feel like a tank, or inside a small hide. A hide is a glorified tent, a cramped torture device which after three hours of having me inside it is in severe danger of being trampled and battered back into its trace elements. Sometimes all of these precautions work, sometimes however it feels like the invisible man couldn't get close enough...

Wild fox cubs like this are incredibly difficult to photograph in the wild as their mothers are on the alert for anything strange like me in the neighbourhood. I didn't see the tongue in this picture until I got it developed, it just adds so much to the cheekiness of the two cubs.

FOUR LITTLE ORPHANS

It had started two days before when a voice on the phone asked *"Andy, how do you fancy raising 4 orphaned fox cubs?"*. Now, two days later, I stood in the enclosure which my next door neighbour Jeff and I had sweated to build, and couldn't wait for them to see it. We'd given them a little woodland, plenty of tunnels and platforms to keep them stimulated and a huge dog kennel to call home. The crate duly arrived, carefully we put it into the enclosure, opened it and waited. After a few minutes a tiny black nose appeared, followed by a pair of furry ears. Then it was out like a flash, straight into the dog kennel, closely followed by its three friends. Little were we to realise how much these four little orphans would change our lives for the next few months.

The next morning I came out to feed them and was greeted by the sight of all four cubs romping round the enclosure having a whale of a time. They were adorable, little bundles of life, and it felt great to see them happy at last after what must have been a traumatic start to their lives.

By August all the foxes were well muscled, healthy and in my opinion stood a good chance of surviving by themselves. Confident that everything was going to plan I left for Scotland to photograph otters; two days later I was back as I'd received a phonecall saying that the foxes had escaped. They'd got tired of our hospitality, and led by the biggest one Boss, had tunnelled out overnight. The first we knew of it was when Jeff next door was out doing the gardening; he'd turned round to get some seeds and found all four cubs sitting there watching him. He almost fell over with the shock.

For the next month they spent their days sleeping in the woods behind our houses; waking up in the early evening to run riot in our gardens. By now, word had spread in the neighbourhood and all available upstairs windows were full by 7pm each evening, waiting for the fox show. The cubs never disappointed, tearing around, pulling apart prize vegetable gardens in the process, before eventually collapsing in a tired heap on our patio. It was great fun but deep inside I knew all this was about to change.

The cubs were mischievous, don't be fooled by that angelic expression, and their stealing from the other gardens seemed to get worse as time went on. Footballs, shuttlecocks, garden implements and gloves, all started to appear in my garden, branding me as the neighbourhood thief! Of course some things were never found, and no doubt future generations will unearth our matching pruning set and think that its a treasured heirloom.

Lady considered the garden her home and could always be found dozing somewhere in the shade, or chasing the Persian cat back into the house.

THE FOX THAT STAYED

One by one all the foxes left us, I was glad that they did as their only chance of survival was to be totally independent. The large vixen, Lady, decided that life was good at No. 75 and stayed with us for the next few months. I'd always had a special bond with her and she would often curl up on the mat inside my office door, or come charging up to me when I was in the garden.

One hot August afternoon I was dozing happily in the sun when I felt a nibble on one of my toes. I slowly opened one eye and saw Lady curled up between my legs. I got up and went inside to get her some food, leaving my thick Sunday newspaper outside. When I came back, Lady was tossing the newspaper around the garden and I decided to leave her to it. I returned a couple of hours later to find the lawn, the rockery and the trees decorated with pieces of Sunday newspaper, whilst an exhausted fox slept on my towel.

Lady had turned into a beautiful fox, with a full red coat and that elegant, inquisitive face. The picture opposite is the last that I ever took of her. As her wild instincts grew she became more and more elusive, until she finally stopped coming at all. For weeks I felt lost and found myself glancing out my office window to see if she was sitting in the garden waiting for me. But she never did return. I took heart from the fact that we'd taken four orphaned cubs that had no chance of any decent life and given them every chance to be independent and survive. It's funny, I've had a very full and exciting life so far, but the days that I spent with Lady were some of the most special moments of my life.

As the Summer wore on Lady became more and more at home in the garden and even took over our favourite seat as her own.

THE WATER GIANTS

Hippos have a great life and I think that rather than being re-incarnated as a football star I'd come back as a Hippo. Imagine, spending 75% of your life either dozing in the sun or floating around on the water, whilst the rest of the time you stuff your face. Yes admittedly I'd be a little on the heavy side but other than that it would be a perfect life. That is until one of your neighbours rolls on top of you during a deep sleep, or some skinny wildlife photographer lurking on the bank opposite tries to take your picture. Oh yes, that's me!

As I watched the herd of hippos I noticed that there were several infants squeezed together between the bulk of their mothers. Hippos, like most mammals, are hyper-protective of their young and to protect them from lions and crocodiles, put them together in the centre of the herd. As they don't have great eyesight, the Hippos couldn't recognise me as human decided instead to assume that I was dangerous. The youngsters were pushed to the back of the herd and I started to get a little nervous when several of the mothers came and stood directly opposite me.

Whilst it may look like Hippos are floating on the water, they are actually standing on the bottom. They prefer shallow water like this so they can chill out and relax without having to worry about drowning. When they sleep, they automatically rise to the surface to breathe, then close their nostrils and fold their ears in to submerge.

The Hippos on the edge of the herd continued to merrily snooze away and I noticed that parts of their skin was becoming red. Hippos have very delicate skin and need to protect it from dehydration and overheating. They do this by secreting a red, oily substance whilst on land, and by taking frequent dips in nearby water. Their skin is also prone to attacks by small insects, so they have a sharing relationship with the local Oxpecker community. The birds get free food, the Hippo gets rid of the annoying tics.

DANGER! WHAT DANGER?

At that point I should have known better and returned to the safety of the truck. For some reason I didn't, and in the next 5 minutes my relationship with the Hippos got progressively worse. A couple of the cows *(and I'm not being derogatory just using their correct name)* lunged into the water downstream from me; I didn't think much of it as they'd been doing the same thing all afternoon to cool themselves down. This time however the two cows swam straight towards me and only stopped when they were 50 ft away. They were now close enough to pose a real threat...

The cows suckle the calves from birth, usually for up to 8 months. To make it easier for the youngster, the cow chooses a part of the river that is very still and not too deep. The calf then folds its ears, closes its nostrils and suckles underneath the water, rising when it needs to breathe.

Warning number one in Hippo language is when they snort and sink below the surface of the water. I was too busy taking pictures to take any real notice of it, next time I'll know better.

All animals usually give a warning before they attack – the rattlesnake "rattles" its tail, a big cat will snarl, and I will climb into a tank. The Hippo has several warnings that it gives before a serious attack, recognising them and their severity is the key to staying alive.

True to the form book, the lead Hippo gave me the first warning. She blew clouds of water in the air through her nostrils, grunted a bit, then sank menacingly underneath the water. For those of you not fluent in hippo speak, this means "I am getting a little annoyed, back off".

DANGER!

After a couple of minutes of silence she served me with the second warning. She opened her mouth to reveal two huge tusks, and from her throat came a prolonged grunt, called a "wheeze-honk" in the trade. The translation this time is "Get lost, I will not warn you again". I don't know why I stayed there. Perhaps I was rooted to the spot, simply stupid or like all men never take no for an answer. The Hippos did give me a final warning when several of them on the bank started wheeze-honking like some quirky choir.

Then it all turned to chaos. The lead Hippo erupted from the water at me, and I caught a glimpse of her huge tusks coming my way. I needed no more warning and ran like a sprinter for the truck. Hippos can easily outrun anyone but at least I had a head start. I made the truck with seconds to spare, vaulted into it and over the other side in one fluid motion. I watched as the hippo stopped some 15 ft from us, her mouth now wide open and those eyes showing some really evil intent. Satisfied that the threat had fled *(it was actually cowering on the other side of the truck)*, she returned to the water. I'd pushed it about as far as I could and only just escaped with my life. Still, that's my job.

The GRIZZLY BEAR

Without doubt, the most dangerous and unpredictable family of animals to photograph, apart from traffic wardens, are bears. You've already read about my exploits with polar bears, well Grizzly Bears have also caused my heart to skip a few beats. I've been in the wrong place at the wrong time three times now, each time I just did what my guides told me – stand still and DON'T look at them. You stand still because Barney bear can outrun *(they can dash to 35 mph)*, outswim and outclimb you and so it's pointless to try. Looking them in the eye is an aggressive move. So you just stand there, clap your hands and shout to identify yourself as human and try to remember all those bear statistics. You know the ones, little gems like 99% of all bear charges are just bluff and the bears don't actually attack you. Maybe its just me, but there is something wrong with that figure. Yes, it's the 1% of bears that do attack that worries me!

American Grizzly or Brown Bears are now confined to the upper parts of the United States, with perhaps the largest population in Alaska.

They are hefty individuals, a big bear that feeds on salmon can weigh over 500 kg. Part of the bears success at adapting to the demands that we put on it, is down to its varied diet.
It can eat over 200 types of plants, small mammals (and large ones), insects, honey and of course salmon. During the summer months it is vitally important that they put on weight for the hibernation ahead, so they stuff about 40 kg of food into their stomachs daily.

One thing that I love about America is that you're always entertained whilst queuing. At Brooks Falls, these bears would put on a really good play fight whilst we were waiting for the float-plane back to the lodge.

The falls are a good place to see the hierarchy that exists in bear land. As you can see the prime fishing spot is occupied by a more dominant bear, forcing the smaller guy to sit and wait.

EXPERT FISHERMEN?

One of my favourite places to watch bears is Brooks Falls in Alaska. Here large groups of Grizzly Bears congregate on a waterfall to watch a platform full of tourists. The bears come to the waterfall during the annual salmon run, as the salmon need to leap the falls to get to their spawning grounds. The tourists come as its great fun to watch Barney the fisherman in action, especially as many of them are rather inept at it. Perhaps the most fun at Brooks Falls is had in the walk to the viewing platform, a $1^1/_2$ mile hike along the bear trail. THE BEAR TRAIL, where bears walk. I loved every minute of it, and even I joined in the clapping and singing when we sighted a bear on the track ahead. For a moment I was even tempted to wear bear bells on my feet, fortunately I was quickly slapped out of it.

It's a tremendous sight to see the bears perching at the top of the waterfall whilst salmon leap all around them.

Some bears are natural born fishermen. They stand on top of the waterfall with their jaws open, lazily waiting for the salmon to leap straight into their mouths. Some however haven't got a clue. Diver is one of these clueless bears, his antics have made him a real favourite with bear voyeurs everywhere.

THE UNLUCKY BEAR

I saw Diver on my first trip to Brooks, and even then I could see his fishing technique was a little flawed. Unlike the rest of the bears who stood on top of the falls, Diver the idiot tried to fish in the white-water underneath them. Every so often he put his head underwater to look for fish, leaving the ridiculous sight of his backside sticking straight up in the air. With all the white, frothy water it must have been impossible to see his paw in front of his face, and after a few seconds he'd surface looking slightly confused and with salmon conspicuous by their absence. He'd look up at the falls mournfully, as he saw the other bears catching more salmon than they could eat.

A bedraggled Diver stares forlornly into the white water, wondering why all the other bears can catch fish and he can't. Perhaps someone should tell him.

With a single deft swish of the head, Grizzlies can go from being absolutely bedraggled to the "shaggy coat" look.

After an hour or so Diver gave up, and walked to the edge of the river. Then, for an instant he looked directly into my lens, his dark eyes boring right into mine, and I was glad I was on a platform. Diver the idiot had returned to being Diver the bear, and he knew it. For a while he hung out by the viewing platform, hoping for another easy meal. The tiny wooden platform was packed, and it threatened to collapse at any moment. I wondered who Diver would choose first, someone with more pork chop on them, or the photographer who had recorded his most embarrassing moments.

T_{HE} O_{RANG} U_{TAN}

Orangutans have wonderfully expressive faces similar in many ways to a human's.

One of my lifelong ambitions has been to photograph Orang Utans in Indonesia. This year, with help from the Orangutan Foundation, my dream came true and I arrived with bags fulls of cameras and an arm full of needles that some sadistic doctor had given me. Two Orang Utans made my trip special, Mono and Christine, these are my diary entries about them.

"I'd followed Rosemarie deep into the jungle; sweat was pouring from my body as it was getting unbearably humid and the mosquitoes were having a field day on my lily-white body. Rosemarie retired to the canopy to make a day nest, her tiny baby Ricard hanging on for dear life underneath her chest. Her older baby, Mono, was so intrigued by his new friends that he stayed and took the prime seat in the house, a branch 3 feet above our heads. So much for our watching wildlife, Mono was watching us".

The name "Orang Utan" means "person of the forest" in the Indonesian language. This "Red Ape" has lived on earth for about 15 million years and is considered the world's oldest great ape. It lives in the jungles of Sumatra and Borneo, where the only variation between the two populations is the shagginess and colour of the coat. Adult males are huge animals and can weigh up to 100 kg. Orangutans have a very varied diet and can eat up to 200 varieties of fruit. They can live to the ripe old age of 40 in the wild.

Mono had a life story that was almost unbelievable for his young years. His real mother had been killed by loggers and he'd been brought to the forest rangers as a tiny baby. At that time Rosemarie had just lost her new baby and was moping about in the area. The rangers placed Mono down in the grass and Rosemarie duly found and adopted him. Now they are inseparable, proof that conservation stories can have happy endings.

Orangutans are great mothers and Rose-Marie was no exception. They are pregnant for nine months, the same as humans, and generally keep their babies close for the first three or so years. Pictures like this are incredibly difficult to get, I was just in the right place at the right time.

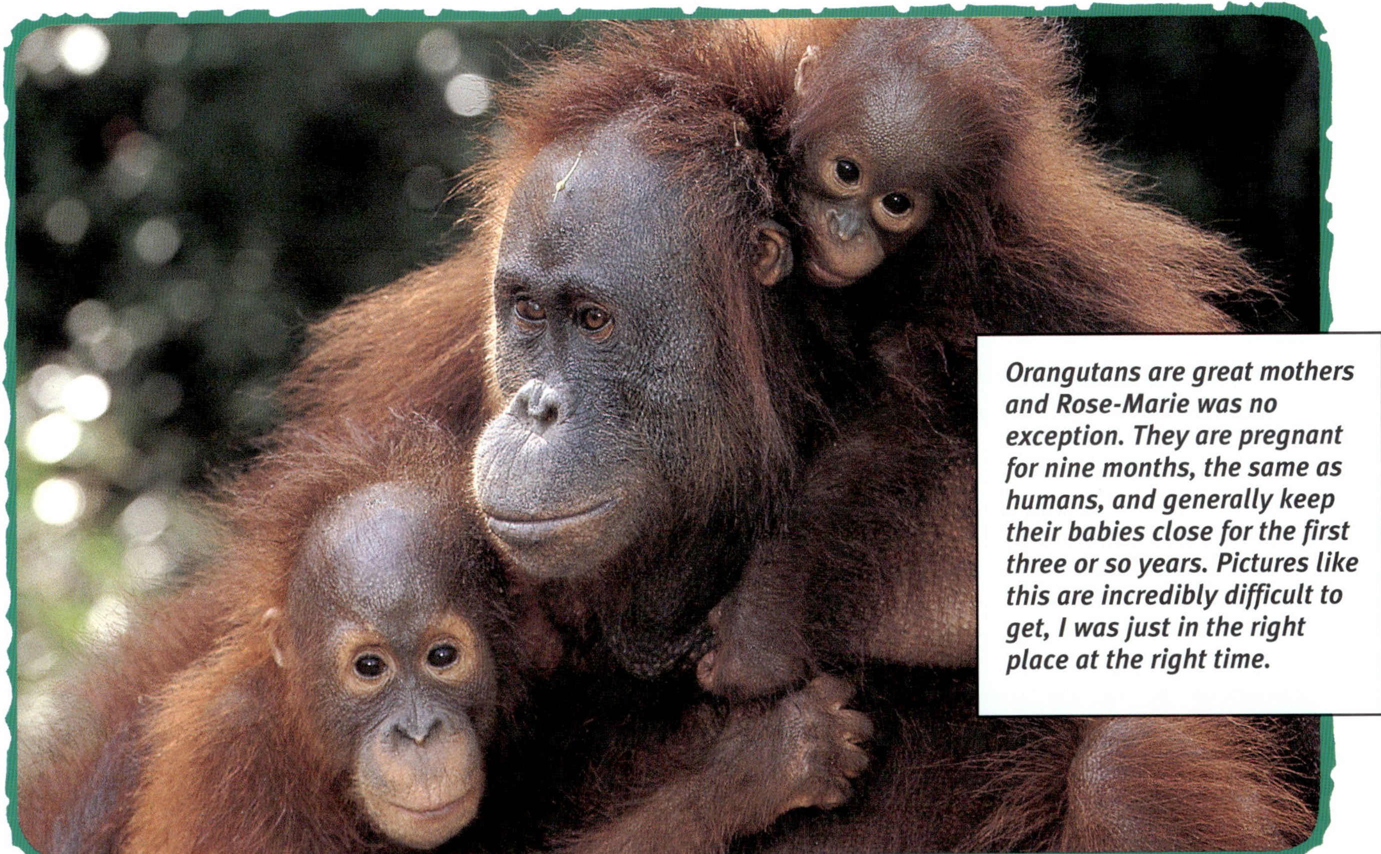

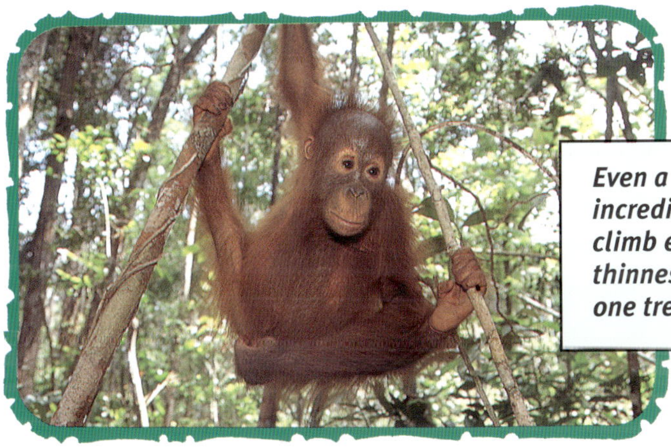

Even a young orangutan is incredibly agile. Mono could climb easily, grabbing the thinnest branches to get from one tree to the next.

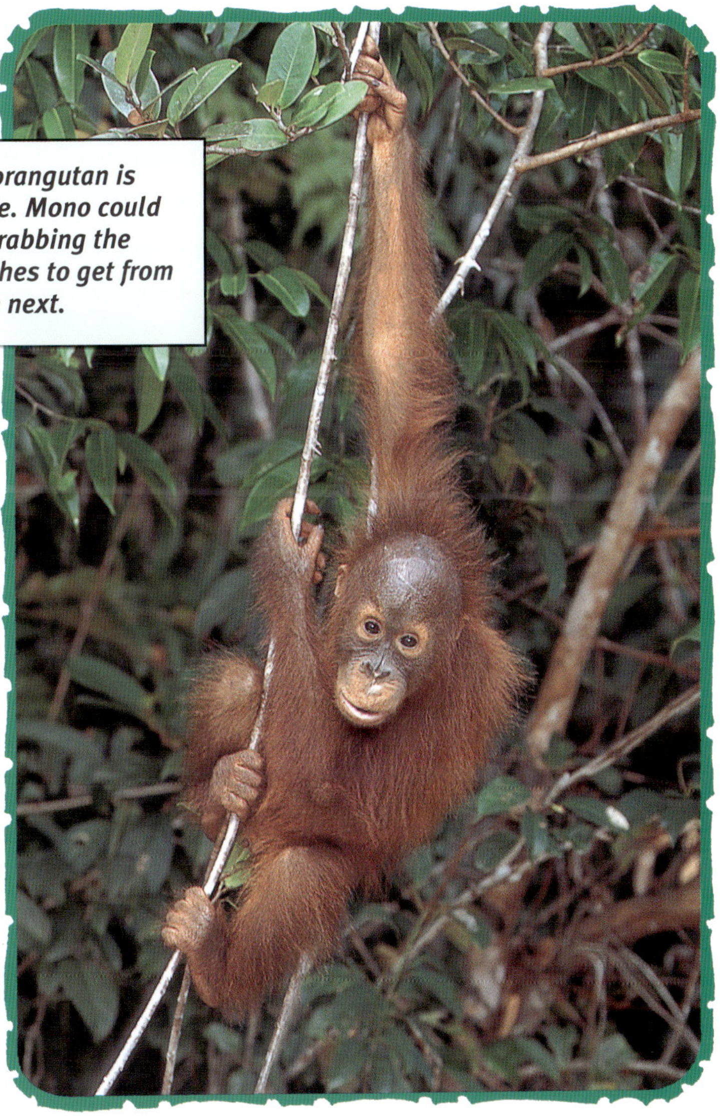

Mono took a keen interest in whatever I did, but he became especially interested in my cameras. When I broke open a new bag of film, the rustle of plastic really got his attention. In a flash he was hanging upside down, reaching out for the offending object. I knew better than to hand over something so dangerous and thought I was doing him a favour by putting it away. But oh no, the little rascal got annoyed and decided to get his own back. First he bombarded me with branches, fruit and anything the little darling could get his hands on. This seemed funny at first, then he grabbed a huge branch and with unbelievable strength started to beat me with it. After a few major whacks to the head I decided that enough was enough and retreated unceremoniously. I've stood my ground to Bull Elephants, Lions and Polar Bears, but this tiny red bundle of fur caused me to run. This is a secret between us, and I trust you not to tell anyone...

Christine and I became close friends, so much so that she washed my hair!

ORANGUTAN HAIRDRESSER

"Today I had my hair washed by an Orangutan! I've spent the day at the rehabilitation clinic started by Dr Birute Galdikas. All the Orangutans were friendly, but with Christine I really clicked. The hair-washing episode started when I was in the wrong place at the wrong time; two other Orangutans had been play fighting and had come crashing down to earth on top of me. A branch whipped across my hand, causing a deep cut which immediately started filling with blood.

Christine, who had been next to me holding my hand, saw the cut and pulled my arm down into some brackish water. She started to wash my hand carefully, then pinched the cut together to stop the bleeding. I was amazed and bent down to get a better look. Big mistake, she saw that my hair was not the cleanest its ever been and decided to wash that too. She pulled me closer to the water and deftly doused my hair with palmfuls of water, until it was soaked. If I'd have had conditioner and a hair dryer I'm sure she would have given me the whole works; I was speechless."

One of the ways that Orangutans show their intelligence is the use of tools to solve problems. One of the Orangutans at Camp Leakey, Princess, knows how to paddle a canoe to get to the other side of the river. Christine showed me her prowess at tool usage by levering bugs out of the ground with a long stick. Temptation then became too much for her and she used the stick to prod another tool, my camera.

By now I hope that you have lived a little of my adventures and been inspired to visit the wonders of the natural world. Through my pictures I hope that you can see how important wildlife is to us, and how essential to our very existence on this planet it is. This book has featured many endangered species, and it is to these that I now want to turn your attention.

The word endangered means threatened, and to all of them there is only one threat to their continued existence, the acts of man. We inherited this planet from them and since then we have systematically cut down their forests, polluted their rivers and hunted them almost to the point of extinction.

The Orangutan is a good example of this. Its forest habitat in Indonesia has been drastically reduced by the effects of logging and illegal clearing by fire consequently its population has plummeted. The Orangutans are innocent bystanders and can do nothing to help themselves, the responsibility lies squarely on our shoulders.

If we don't start acting soon, then this endearing picture of Christine will be just a memory, a page in a book which future generations will marvel over, from inside a concrete world.

Throughout this book there will two groups of people; those of you that say "oh my god, why did he do that" and those that say "oh my god, how did he do that". For the first group I hope to have an answer before I get eaten by something, for the rest of you this is your page. It's easy to get over technical here and talk f-stops, exposures and all that stuff, there I've even done it, but I want this section to be inspirational not dull and boring. Firstly it doesn't matter if you've got the top of the range camera or the bottom, the basic ability to take a good photograph depends on the way you see things. Sure I have expensive gear but it's my job and I have to sell pictures in a very very competitive business against the best wildlife photographers in the world. It's much better to take the time to learn about your subject and its behaviour, than to waste time having to learn all the fancy (and invariably useless) gizmos on your camera. I hope that the examples below will show you a little of my thought processes when taking the pictures in this book.

The most striking thing about this picture is the distorted perspective of the elephant against the background. I achieved this by using an ultra-wide angle lens, a 17mm in fact, which if you remember was triggered remotely. Modern wildlife photography books always seem to recommend buying the biggest lens that you can, I hope that you can see that this isn't always necessary.

Equipment Used : Canon EOS 5 Body, 17-35mm lens, 81A Warm-up filter, LC-3 Remote trigger, Fuji Velvia film, Nescafè Gold Blend, a bucket of water.

It is very rare that I get an animal in bright sunlight and so I have learnt various ways to improve my chances of getting a sharp picture in less than perfect conditions. This Polar Bear shot was a prime example. The sun had set 30 minutes previously and the light that you see on the bear was an afterglow. The biggest enemy with low light is shutter speed, so you want to keep it as high as you can; the easiest way of doing this is to put your camera on aperture priority mode and select the lowest value (usually f4 or f5.6) which automatically selects the fastest shutter speed, trust me. Anyway I set mine to f4, took a light reading from my hand held meter and got a shutter speed of 1/30th sec. This was a little slow, so to increase it to 1/60th sec. I pushed my 100 ASA film to 200. Other than that I used an image stabiliser lens to reduce the camera shake and balanced the whole lot on a very firm bean bag.

Equipment Used: Canon EOS5 body, 300mm F4L Image Stabiliser lens, 81A warm-up filter, Fuji Provia 100 film pushed to 200.

Sometimes I'm forced to take pictures in the heat of the day, when the sun is at its highest and the shadows are harsh. When taking this Caiman shot, I darkened the background exposure by 1/2 stop and used a fill-in flash to both highlight the Caiman against it and remove any annoying shadows. The flash power was reduced by -2 stops as I was very close to the Caiman, and I used an additional diffuser to create the soft lighting effect on the skin. I used the same fill-in flash shots with the Snow Monkey in the geothermal pool (p71) and all the orangutan pictures.

Equipment Used: Canon EOS1N HS body, 17-35mm lens, 81A warm-up filter, Canon 540EZ Speedlite flashgun mounted on Quantum off-camera bracket, Quantum Turbo battery, Fuji Provia 100 film.

If you are going to use a wide-angle lens then I think that it is essential that you use an 81A warm-up filter in conjunction with it. The term "warm-up" is a bit of a red-herring, sure it does improve the orange tone of the picture but I use it to cut down glare and create a saturated sky as you see here. This picture was taken at midday, without the filter it would have been a wishy-washy light blue colour. Urghhh.

Equipment Used: Canon EOS1N HS body, 17-35mm lens, 81A warm-up filter, Fuji Velvia film.

Taking action pictures has always been my speciality and these Japanese Cranes tested my ability to the limit. To freeze their dancing I set my camera to aperture priority (AV) and an aperture of f5.6, which I knew would give me a very fast shutter speed. I could have got an even faster shutter speed by setting the aperture to f4 but the Cranes had a habit of jumping away from each other and I was worried about the depth of field. The background was very distracting and the autofocus had a habit of tracking onto it at the wrong moment, so I manually focused the lens on the left hand crane and let my depth of field bring the right hand one into sharp focus.

Equipment Used: Canon EOS3 body, 600mm F4L lens with 1.4x teleconverter, 81A warm-up filter, Fuji Provia 100 film.

Once you have mastered the basics of exposure, it then becomes your friend and allows you to do a little creative stuff. The first picture above shows a polar bear in a snow-storm. To accentuate the white-out effect of the storm, I overexposed this picture by +1 stop from the "correct" reading. The second picture shows a polar bear sleeping and for this I did the opposite. To create a mood indicating an evening snooze, I underexposed (darkened) by -2/3 stop from the "correct" reading. This picture also shows the benefits of shooting with a wide-angle lens at a high depth of field (F16 here), as the habitat is beautifully sharp and leads the eye into the polar bear.

Equipment Used: Canon EOS1N HS body, 600mm F4L lens for snowstorm, 70-200f2.8L lens for iceberg, , 81A warm-up filter, Gitzo Mountaineer tripod, cable release, Fuji Velvia film.

Exposure problems are always caused by water, white water makes it a nightmare. When Diver sat underneath the waterfall my camera gave a ridiculous exposure reading of 1/4000th at f5.6 for 50 ASA film. I looked up to check the sun hadn't exploded, and satisfied that I wasn't being cooked alive, sat down and thought about the correct way to expose the picture. The camera was being fooled by the bright water, and it was no good taking a reading from his fur as it was dark and would give an incorrect reading the other way. In the end I decided that the sunlight on me was the same as on him (it was directly over my shoulder) and so took a reading from the wooden platform I was standing on, as that was a very medium tone. I then bracketed 1/2 stop around this value, the result is what you see here.

Equipment Used: Canon EOS5 body, 600mm F4L Lens, Fuji Provia 100 film, Gitzo Mountaineer tripod.

Thanks to my guides
Gavin, Arne, Harry, David, John and Sharyn
and for their encouragement
Tim, Mark and Sheena from NHPA
David Hill, Martin Carter, Andrew Jackson
for his inspiration Cherry Kearton
the first wildlife photographer

Animal Tales
First Edition © September 1999
Published by
2M PUBLISHING LTD
Shamrock House
Woodbury Park Road
Royal Tunbridge Wells
Kent TN4 9NQ

Telephone: 01892 545959

Photographs & Text
ANDY ROUSE

Design & Art Direction
GRANT BRADFORD

Cartoons
SOOZI

Page Planning
TONY SAMBROOK
REX CARR

Colour Reproduction & Printing
Midas Printing Ltd Hong Kong

ISBN 0 9536335 0 0

Visit Andy's website
www.andyrouse.co.uk
for more details of photographs and future
TV, video and other adventures.